Naturally Magical

The Workbook to Reclaim Your Magic

Richard Allen Griggs

GREEN MAGIC

Green Magic
53 Brooks Road
Street
Somerset
BA16 0PP
England

www.greenmagicpublishing.com

Designed & typeset by K.DESIGN
Winscombe, Somerset

ISBN 9781838418502

GREEN MAGIC

Disclaimer

Everyone is naturally magical. What is <u>already</u> magical about you? You can employ this workbook to find out. Each workbook exercise, called a journey, helps you to unleash your inner magician, and the results are recorded in a magic journal. Upon completing all 35 journeys, you will have in your hands a guide to your personal brand of magic. Since this is your journey, the author cannot take responsibility for what you discover, practice or document as magic.

Contents

Part Three: Design Magic Rituals   109

INTRODUCTION

LAUNCHING THE JOURNEY

CHAPTER ONE

Let's Get Started!

Did you ever, if only as a child, long to practice magic? I believe such yearnings are neither theatrical nor mystical. Rather, they are a natural and ancient part of being human. Can you sense the magic within yourself? Do you feel naturally magical? Do you want to build upon that? If so, I have designed this workbook to help you recover the magic that lies dormant within you.

If nature is the source of magic (it is) and if you are part of nature (you are), then magic is already in your nature. You can find that nature by looking within. The purpose of this workbook is to take you on an introspective journey wherein you discover the precise ways in which you are magical. This workbook helps you to look within to question the injunctions that stop you from knowing about or practicing *your* magic. It also has you experimenting with magic to discover the ways that suit only you. You are lightly guided so that your own creative juices are stimulated and flow into the design of powerful rituals.

Billions of us, the masses, who were taught just enough to do our jobs and pay our taxes, lost track of the magic that fulfilled human lives for nearly all of history. In recent centuries, our magic light dimmed so much that most people now think of magic as theatre or pulling rabbits out of hats. If you feel, see, or sense the magic within you and want it back, then I wrote this workbook for you. It might be the only workbook available on reclaiming the magic that is hidden inside you. You use the magic already within your character to build a practice.

The Workbook Formula:
Guided Introspection and a Journey

Each chapter has two parts. The first part, which I call guided introspection, is a combination of questions, prose, stories, ideas, logic, tips and practices that provide the inspiration for a journey of self-discovery. I am not 'training' you but guiding you into introspection by asking questions and sharing my experiences. If I trained or instructed you in the practice of magic, you would not be discovering it through an introspective process.

After you read the chapter narrative stimulating inner reflections, you arrive at the journey, the workbook exercise wherein you experiment to discover your natural magic, always independent of me. You capture your findings in a magic journal, either hardbound or digital. Upon completing this journal, you will have a guide to your personal brand of magic, including tools, practices and rituals.

Why this Formula Works

Here are four reasons why the described workbook formula takes you on a path to finding the magician within:

★   Magic is already within you from birth. It is in the materials of which you and the cosmos are made, including earth (matter), air (atmosphere), fire (sun), water (liquid) and spirit (space). For example, a pineal gland or 'third eye' exists as part of the human genome that enables magicians to see into the spirit world. That suggests to me that magic has been part of our evolutionary path for a very long time

★   If you come to question, within your own being, the indoctrination, laws, injunctions, rules, belief systems, and programming that keep you unaware of your magical capacities, you gain a way to reclaim your magic

★   Introspection helps you to identify the magical ways that fit with who you are as a character (your character *is* the source of your magic, especially considering this is practical magic)

★   Lastly, by looking within, you will see that magic is not something elite, esoteric, or requiring a mentor. Rather, the basic thesis here (contested in some quarters) is that *magic is completely human and natural but has been suppressed.* I want to lift feet off shoulders by helping others to find their own magic

The Author's Role in Your Journey

The workbook's underlying premise is that you are already a unique character and therefore magical. I help you to introspect and unleash that magical self. So, do not think of me as your teacher, master, or guru because this is your journey, and you are in the driver's seat. Next to you, as a friendly guide, I help you to navigate past the curves, wrong turns, blind corners, mistaken notions, injunctions and tricky indoctrination that must be overcome on this less travelled road to magic. Second, I review some tools of practice, which you can take or leave. Finally, I guide you into designing rituals, the way magicians get things done.

Practical Magic

This workbook falls under the category of practical magic. Individuals, like myself, who practice on their own (belonging to no covens, schools, or groups) are known as *practical magicians*. Within practical magic, there are as many different practices as there are practitioners. There is no need to agree with one another as to how to practice magic, which tells you why I am not offering myself as a role model. This is a self-discovery approach. I will show you many ways to be more of your magical self! The more you are you, the more magical you become, and the more you design magic practices to fit with who you are as a character (a more powerful approach than copying someone else).

A Little Bit About Me

Since this is a workbook that helps you to design your own practice, I do not want you to copy my magic. I just want to share the path that I took to discover my own magic practice. However, I must offer you some examples of practice now and again and these will necessarily come from my experiences. So, let me tell you a wee bit about my magic ways so that you can learn to distinguish mine from yours.

I seek harmonious relations between myself and the life-giving energies of the Cosmos: earth, air, fire, water, and spirit. I have, at times, called that elemental magic, nature magic, or natural magic. However, such names do not matter because I am just a practical magician doing my own thing and not following any school. I also studied indigenous people's geography formally (PhD, University of California, Berkeley 1993) and strongly relate to certain indigenous perspectives on magic (e.g. Native American, Aboriginal). However, I also appreciate European traditions such as making use of a magic journal as a way to document and improve practice. Sharing such ways gives you examples of practice and methods to try out but there is no expectation that your magic should be like mine.

Schools of Magic

Just like science is a generic term for many different disciplines (e.g. biology, chemistry or geology), magic is a categorical term for many different schools (e.g. shamanism, paganism, witchcraft, ancestral, metaphysics, sorcery, wizardry, animism, ceremonial, illusionary or folk). What practitioners mean by any of these words varies tremendously. In practical magic, the source of magic is your character rather than a set of teachings or a school. Rather, each practitioner is a whole school! So, in this workbook, the full expression of your natural character is treated as completely magical.

The Three Workbook Sections

There are three main sections in this workbook: (1) Reclaim Your Magic; (2) Learn Magic Practices; and (3) Design a Magic Practice.

Section One helps you to question certain myths that stop you from ever knowing about or practicing magic. One must debunk many injunctions (myths we buy into) that blind us to both the existence of magic and its practice. To encourage such an introspective journey, Section One of the workbook is in a 'question and answer' format.

Section Two familiarizes you with some rather common practices within the magic community that you may or may not want to employ in designing a practice. Techniques like dancing to lift your spirit, projecting colors from your aura for protection, or using the power of imagination to manifest a wish are examples of practices that will be briefly explored in this section. Section Two presents a toolbox for your perusal without insisting that you include all of them in your practice. Rather, select some of the tools, all of them, or reject them all. However, if you reject them all (unlikely), you will need to find techniques that you can integrate into the design of rituals in Section Three.

In Section Three, you integrate some Section Two tools (or others that you find) into the design of rituals, the way magicians get things done. The only rule to which you must adhere is in a very ancient motto pertaining to magic: 'first, do no harm.' That means you are not trying to change, hurt or convert! You are just doing your own thing.

Keeping a Magic Journal

Many magicians record their practices in magic workbooks or journals (known by some as grimoires). Such journals document magic practices that did or did not work. Thus, magicians improve over time by documenting and reviewing practice. They constantly improve their magic journals, filling them up with so many scribbles and fly-away notes that eventually they start a new one!

The entries in your journal are not homework like in school. Rather, they are steps toward identifying and documenting the magic ways suiting only you. You walk away from this workbook as a practicing magician with all tools, practices and successes documented in a magic journal that is unique to you. That vision of setting out to explore your own magical tendencies, you must keep in mind to employ the workbook successfully. The source of your magic is you.

Tips on Getting the Most Out of this Workbook

I have three tips as to how to employ this workbook successfully:

★ Reading about magic will not turn you into a magician. Practice will. The workbook was designed to help you rediscover your inner magician through both introspection and practice. So, if you want powerful results, take each journey in the order given, resting overnight between lessons

★ Most of us have been taught to present a 'positive' face to the world but each one of us, like a battery, is positively and negatively charged. To get your magic spark, it is essential that you come to know, equally well, both the characteristics that you positively express and those that you repress within your character. To become a magician, you must know yourself, warts and all

★ To find magic by deprogramming (part of the aim of this workbook), you must question some widespread propaganda and socialization, which can make people around you feel threatened. To avoid defending every step of a highly personal transformation with fellows and friends, I would not share much about your journey until you have completed the workbook

The Pace to Completion

The best pace is to take it slow and in chapter order. The chapters are short and plainly written but packed with magic wisdom. The style is easy-to-read. However, I put some big concepts into plain language. So, please take it slow, pausing to reflect on each chapter sub-heading, before moving onto the next. A slow pace is better for your self-discovery of magic. In fact, take a night's rest between lessons, because sleep, dreams and the subconscious mind can transform the day's learning into a heightened state of consciousness.

If a lesson is easy to complete or if you are enjoying the journey, do another one the next day. If a chapter is challenging, take up to a week on it but no longer because interest and discipline wane at a slower pace. If you want to schedule your lessons onto a calendar, do so based on the times and days per week that you are available for a one-hour session.

★ JOURNEY 1 ★

Each journey must be documented in an eye-pleasing journal, a record of how you understand magic and your practices. Please design a magic journal that is both attractive and well suited to your character. If you make it magical, it will add magic to your learning experience. Your first entry will be a photograph (or drawing) of yourself and a self-description.

Do you want a quick and easy way to start a magic journal? Liking the convenience of a computer and being a fast typist, I set up a title page on my Mac, illustrated it with a wand and gave it a temporary title (Reclaim the Magician Within) and got going. I worked on the design elements over time.

You could also consider an old-fashioned grimoire; a magician's manual, that you can hold in your hand. You could recover the outside of an old binder, but it must contain some 200 pages that can be inserted and removed as needed because corrections, changes and additions will arise. This hardcopy would require a designed cover page. You could design the cover to express something unique about you since your unique character is the source of your magic. A computer word program offers an easy way to make entries, print them out, and paste them into a journal. That enables you to double-capture your entries in both electronic and hardcopy versions, which is the best of both worlds: an old-fashioned grimoire you can take anywhere and a back-up on your computer!

Do you want to be creative and think outside the box? You can consider any medium that suits you, like audio or video recordings. Some might use their phone. Just bear in mind that, at times, you need to insert or capture photographs, sketches, diagrams and illustrations. Since it is very likely you will revise and edit your magic guide continuously, even after the course, consider in design what will be easiest for you in the long-term and not just the short-term. Creativity is not being ruled out, however. Shine your light!

When the journal is completed, take a close-up photograph of your face (frontal), print it out and enter it into your journal. Alternatively, depending on your skills, you can also use a mirror and sketch a self-portrait into your journal. Now, analyze every feature from ear-to-ear and head-to-chin — what do your facial features reveal to you about your character?

What should you observe? Enter into a magical state of self-reflection. Take the time to ask the right questions. Is your face thoughtful, fiery, earthy, spiritual, or full of emotion? Do you have the face of an innocent? Are you proud or humble? Are you kind or harsh? Are you free-spirited or in control? Are you marked in some way by the tensions of the past? What personal history shows in your face? What beliefs are there in your eyes and lips? What strengths do you see? What vulnerabilities? What magic?

Can you be specific, accurate and honest with yourself? Taking a neutral look at yourself in the mirror unlocks many doors to magic. Document what you see in your journal well because this exercise will be repeated at the end of this workbook to demonstrate the progress that you made in finding your inner magician. The photo also provides a reference point for you in the upcoming six chapters as you seek to document the elemental mix that describes your unique character. Be sure to calendar date every entry and number each page as this helps to locate passages and materials as the journal gets thicker.

★ PART ONE ★

FACE YOUR MAGIC

Part One asks you to introspect and reclaim your inner magic. To raise matters for introspection, the chapter narratives are in 'question-and-answer' format as if you were asking the question. So, carefully consider each question and then read the narrative for inspiration. Then, at the end of the chapter, take a journey wherein you discover magic independent of me.

CHAPTER TWO

DISCOVER YOUR ELEMENTAL MIX

Earth, water, air, fire and spirit describe an elixir without which there would be neither life nor magic. All five elements are in every living thing but in different proportions, such that we can use the five elements to describe anything from the cells in your body to the entire universe. The purpose of next seven chapters: what mix of these elements best describes your character?

What is Meant by an Elemental Mix?

I am not speaking of the 118 elements on the periodical table, as discussed by scientists, but of five life-giving elements; energies as alive as ourselves. Many of us see them as gods and goddesses responsible for life, rather than impersonal forces. We can commune with them to expand awareness, promote harmony, create joy, induce peace and spread love.

Can the Elements Describe my Character?

Yes. I do empathic readings where I routinely use the elements to describe general tendencies in a person's character and it works like a charm. Two elements usually dominate a person's character although every combination is possible. One might have two strong elements, like air-earth (intellectual but grounded) and thirdly fire (passionate) but much weaker of water (feeling) or spirit (connection). Another might be strong in heart and spirit and weak in air, earth and fire. We will review all possible combinations but knowing your own elemental mix, how the proportion and expression of them might describe your character, offers you a way to better understand yourself, which is the key source of your magic.

Does my Elemental Mix Mean that I Fall into a Category?

Your elemental composition does not put you into a category. The elements are not like astrological signs. Your elemental composition is only a point along the magical journey that your soul is taking. You might be air-based (a thinker) today and then evolve over the years toward being a more water-based person (a feeling person). Two people of the same elemental composition are not identical but share some tendencies. People also mature over time. For example, a space/heart type might be distant and confused at 20 but mature into a great visionary at 45.

What do you Mean by 'Strong' in One Element and 'Weak' in Another?

I have never met someone with five equally strong elements. For instance, someone might have one very strong element that dominates the other four like someone who is all heart. Our weaknesses are as important as our strengths. Once alert to our weaknesses, we are much stronger than when we denied them. Seeing that we are not perfect but have both character faults *and* weaknesses helps round out our characters. For instance, we are kinder to others when we see the flaws in ourselves. You cannot correct weaknesses or compensate for them if you deny that they exist.

How do I Benefit from Knowing my Elemental Composition?

You, as a character, have a unique elemental mix. Knowing one's own elemental composition creates self-awareness and a way to identify and correct imbalances. You already commune with certain elements to strengthen yourself but might not be conscious of it. Every day of your life, you drink water when thirsty, eat when hungry, breathe oxygen by the second, seek warmth when cold and long for a spiritual connection to this world although you might not be fully conscious of it. Do you really need me or a scientific study or some authority to tell you that the elements can bring healing and balance when you are already doing it or longing for them, perhaps unconsciously, all day every day? Rather, take the magical path of becoming more conscious of the elements that give you life.

How Can I Find My Elemental Mix?

Self-reflection is the best way to discover your elemental mix, but the journey can be a little tricky. Let me warn you of some traps. The main one is imagining yourself to be different than who you really are (owing to socialization or ego). Your elemental mix is not how you have been raised, hurt, or what you want to be but describes your underlying character, how you characteristically adapt or adjust to the world. Do not compare the elements to astrological signs, as your elemental mix is:

★ Based on five elements and not four

★ Found by looking within rather than to the stars

★ A mixture of elements rather than a sun sign

★ Changeable from birth to death

Can I Read Anyone's Elemental Mix?

Reading someone else's elemental mix takes practice, as one makes mistakes while learning. Imagine a man who is reluctant to share very deep feelings with you. His reticence might be misread as lacking in heart, but he might be so big-hearted and feel so vulnerable in the wrong company that he is very shy at first. Imagine a very thoughtful woman who *describes in words*, rather than expressing in tears, the sadness she feels. You might read her as heart, but she is more likely to be air (verbal, thoughtful). To avoid such confusion, I look straight into the eyes and read the alchemical mix but that took years of practice. However, if someone is fiery, I will see that fire right in their eyes. How does one practice? Start by observing yourself (today's journey)!

21

Can you Guide me?

Let's identify one primary element in your character right now. What excites the real you, the inner magician? Magic is much about locating your joy. Are you most excited about earthy matters: nature, your home, your income, plants, herbs, animals or land? Then, you are earth. Are you mainly a thinker inspired by logic, well-reasoned arguments and good explanation? Then, you are air. Are you focused most of the time on spiritual growth (or imagining a better world) and do you find rampant materialism irritating? Then, you are space/spirit (we will review the distinction just below). Do you value feelings above thoughts, read emotions without words being spoken and find yourself attracted to animals? Then, you are heart. Are you passionate? Do you focus on those things that get your fire going, like romance, travel and fame? Do you like to influence a crowd? Are you a natural warrior? Then, you are fire.

What do you Mean by Spirit/Space?
Which One is it?

Of the five elements, spirit/space might be the trickiest one to comprehend because our beliefs play a role in which of these two terms we prefer. Do you believe in God or that a living spirit imbues all things with life? If you say 'yes', you might prefer to speak of spirit. Do we live in a materialist universe where space is physical fabric that is 'cut' by light to create form? If you say 'yes', then you might speak of space.

In this volume I am comfortable with either term (spirit or space). The term space tells us it is a real substance just like Einstein said and not an empty void (the weight of planets displacing space like a ship displacing water in the ocean). Spirit is the more commonplace term in the magic community, and I mainly defer to that. However, the term that you use is for you to decide and not me. I do not seek to convert you to a belief system but to help you discover your naturally magical ways. So, you will have to choose your preferred term or use both (dependent on context), like me.

Can you Illustrate the Five Elements?

The illustration on the next page offers another way for you to decide upon your elemental mix. Review it slowly. There is no need to define your elemental mix in a rush as ahead you have six chapters of narrative and exercises to assist you.

FIVE ELEMENTS IN DESCRIBING HUMAN CHARACTER

Correspondences ↓

Air/Thought (East)	Fire/Passion (South)	Earth/Matter (North)	Water/Heart (West)	Spirit/Space (All directions)
Sees the living atmosphere as home	Seeks romance and romantic settings	At home in nature	Seeks closeness to water bodies	Feels a kinship with the Cosmos
Attracted to open air	Loves the sun and stars	Thinking grounded in 'reality'	A feeler; deep emotions	Imaginative
Uses air to purify and heal	Sees fire as the energy behind motion; the way to get things done	Likes earthy comforts	High emotional intelligence	Peers upward into space to stimulate the imagination
Very compatible with earth people	Passionate and a doer who inspires others	Connects well to plants	Dissipates anxiety with water (tea, a shower, a swim)	Often intuitive
Employs air to remove stale and dark energy and reduce anxiety	Uses fire to heal, purify and destroy	Often focused on fertility — motherhood, crops, regenerating the earth	Highly adaptable (water is fluid)	Heals self by making the unconscious conscious
Very sensitive to atmospheric changes and music	Regenerates and renews with fire	Loves trees and fears fire	Uses water to purify and heal	Interested in spatial arrangement and ordering
Opens windows to revitalize thinking	Keen on sight: seeing is believing	Heals the body in earthy ways	Feels a strong kinship with all life	Finds calm in spirituality
Strong sense of direction	Mercurial (moody)	Loves food, nutrition	Loyal and highly committed	Loves the big picture
A thinker, verbal	Loves an audience	Love is physically expressed	Needs downtime to protect and heal the heart	Might conflict with the less imaginative air or earth people
Might conflict with water or fire people (thought vs. emotions or passions)	Might conflict with anyone not understanding romance, passion	Might conflict with space people (not grounded enough)	Might conflict with air people who are seldom as heart-sensitive	

What are the Correspondences?

The correspondences shown on the table (air and thought, fire and passion, earth and matter, heart and water, and spirit & space) speak of influences on character. For example, the water person, above all else, is heart-based. The earth person tends to dwell on material matters. The air person tends toward a world of thoughts. The fire person is full of passion. The spirit person is the most imaginative.

How Can the Five Elements Help me to Find Magic?

Magic starts with understanding what you find worthy of worship. May I suggest some things that are worthy of worship? There would be no magic without the elements because there would be no life. To worship them is to express gratitude for life, which builds joy from within, renders the powers to heal, helps with manifestation, engenders peace and creates inner tranquility. If I feel out of balance, I can worship the missing element to bring it into my being (invocation). That example also reveals a bit about magic, which is less about snapping your fingers and saying 'voila!' than a disciplined activity, albeit fun, requiring regular practice.

★ JOURNEY 2 ★

The five elements are always with us. Wherever you are and at any time, you can honor, observe, value and appreciate all five elements. This journey asks you to discover the elements in your home. I want you to list, map, sketch or illustrate in any fashion the mix of elements per main spaces of your home and then to evaluate your elemental mix in terms of where you experience the most comfort. If your favorite spot is outside in the sun, what does that say about you? You could either be a person of fire (like attracts like) or lacking fire (opposites attract too). If you are highly attracted to water features (swimming pools, bathtubs, showers) you might be a water person or not. You have to observe how and why you are attracted.

Each room in your house has its own elemental composition. So, this is a fun and useful learning experience, offering clues to your elemental mix. Do not worry if, upon completion of this journey, you are still unsure. This is an educational exercise too. By the time you finish Chapter Seven, you will have clearly decided which elements are dominant or subordinate in your character.

Becoming more aware of the elements around you, can help you to correct imbalances within your being (feelings of disharmony) or outside of it (atmospheric disharmony in place). Places that seem too watery, spacey, fiery, earthy or atmospheric or lacking an element, can be corrected. One can add a water feature to bring balance to a spot that is too fiery. So, while taking this journey, feel free to respond to your findings and improve the elemental harmony in your home where you can. For instance, if not too fiery yourself, you might open more spaces up to the sun to improve the elemental balance (you feel it). Just remember to document those findings and responses in your journal.

Here are the three parts of today's journey:

PART ONE: Illustrate or describe the type of elemental dominance you find in the main rooms/spaces of your home. In other words, try to label rooms or significant spaces just as you would describe a person's elemental mix. To do this, you could head five consecutive journal pages each with the name of a room and describe the elemental mix in each OR map this out in your journal using a floor plan.

For many, the kitchen might seem fire-dominant (electricity, appliances, stove) but it also contains water (sink, foods, beverages) and earth (food, furnishings). The bathroom might be the most water-dominant (think of sinks, bathtubs, or toilets). You might have gardens (earth, water), windows (fire, air), fireplaces (fire), overhead lighting (fire), outside areas open to the night sky (space) or certain spacious areas where there is room to move around freely (space).

PART TWO: Of those mapped places, identify where you feel most comfortable or free to be yourself. Do you feel most comfortable in those places where fire touches your face or body (e.g. a sunny room, or by the fireplace at night)? You might be attracted to fire then. If it soothes you, it might be something elemental in your character or otherwise missing and only you can work that out. You might also feel 'in your element' where your imagination can wander. Then, likely you live from the spirit and are creative. You might feel great in very *private* spaces like an office, bedroom, attic, or even outside under the sun or stars where you can express yourself undisturbed. Do you feel liberated when you can connect to the stirrings of your own heart – a place next to your pets or perhaps luxuriating in the bathtub (*water*)? Do you naturally gravitate toward the earthy areas of your home (e.g. garden, kitchen) where there might be soil, comfort foods, or herbs (*earth*)? Is it airiness that you like, where fresh breezes circulate or where you can oxygenate with exercise, dance, or movement?

PART THREE: Use your maps, drawings, sketches, notes and findings regarding your elemental mix to complete a dated journal entry. First, illustrate what you found in terms of the most and least relaxing areas of the house. Second, explain what this journey taught you, even if it was not conclusive about your elemental mix. Third, did you do anything magical to adjust the elemental mix in areas that are less relaxing? Fourth, did you discover anything magical about your dwelling or at least how to create more magic for yourself in your home environment?

CHAPTER THREE

ARE YOU WATER-DOMINANT?

Water is a living goddess, an intelligence that flows throughout the entire human body 24/7 without stop. One of our biggest bodily organs; the heart, regulates, moves, and pumps a river of liquid nutrients through thousands of miles of blood vessels to nourish every cell. Every second of the day, we respond to feeling, touch, emotion, sensation, love and connection; all sourced in water. The huge amount of unfiltered and authentic information being gathered this way, by the second, is so huge and immediate that we take it for granted, seldom stopping to fully appreciate water as a living intelligence.

What are Some Characteristics of Water-Dominant People?

Perhaps the key feature of water-based people is that they are centered in their hearts, rather than their heads. We can speak of heart-based people as water-based and vice-versa. They treasure pure communication from the heart and are champions of heart-based understanding and expression. Most of them share what they feel as they feel it. Even the most reserved water-based people tend to expose exactly what they are feeling in unaffected and easy-to-read facial expressions! Water-based people are so emotionally honest and so averse to censoring feelings, that their faces can tell us what rings true. Such authenticity attracts many warm people into their lives.

Some water-based people are empathic. They rely more on heart-intelligence than intellect although they can have fine minds too. However, by being in touch with their authentic feelings, they gather a vast amount of accurate information about the world around them. Some become psychics (the heart is a field of energy!) who offer readings straight from the heart at high speed without any discussion, information or fact checking. They might read the hearts of total strangers and stream out wisdom warranting serious reflection.

What Kinds of Challenges do Water-Dominant People Face?

Water-based people, with faces that never lie, have a big challenge. Owing to their emotional expressiveness or the authentic look on their faces, they unwittingly expose and upset those who are emotionally repressed. That explains why many empaths, who are naturally kind people, spend long periods alone, hiding away from the world. Rather than being unfriendly, they are too kind and authentic for a game-playing world.

Water-based people are forced to confront another dilemma: societies based on conformity. If they suppress their hearts to conform to societal dictates, it might make life a little easier, but they lose their psychic gift in the process. So, to retain their high level of sensitivity, water-based people have to manage their gift. Many of them are private, spend little time in public spaces and are very discerning about the company they keep. Alone time often becomes the best friend of water-based people. Other techniques include time in the sun, dance, bathing in herbs and particular rituals to be covered in other chapters.

Who is Typically Compatible with the Water-Dominant Person?

Water-based people make friends quite easily with fire-based people who, like dragons, will defend their sensitive heart-based friends. In turn, a water-based person can also bring a measure of calm to the passionate fire-based person. Since fire people understand passion, they relate to the compassionate nature of the heart-based ones. Just like it sounds, fire and water can produce a 'steamy' relationship!

That natural compatibility between the fire and water people does not mean that earth-based or air-based people do not bring calm to people of the heart as well. However, under certain circumstances, a natural kind of conflict can arise. Water-based types connect to the world in a fluid, organic, and serendipitous way, involving feeling and compassion, while the air-based types often subdue emotion so they can negotiate the world more factually. So, the fluidity of water people can alarm air people who want 'cut and dried' facts. Of course, there are people of a water-air mix who have deep feelings but articulate them in words rather than just expressing raw emotions.

What is the Ideal Environment for Water-Dominant People?

As warriors of the heart, many young water-based people volunteer to help the downtrodden, sick, poor, wounded or aged. Many public servants such as teachers, nurses and rescue personnel will be heart-based people. Such passions can see them slow to settle down. Once they do, we find many of them living near water bodies such as coastlines, lakes, streams and ponds. Many water-earth types gravitate to farms where fresh-water streams feed the land. People of a water-spirit combination might settle along a coastline for that big overview.

How do the Other Elements Influence a Water-Dominant Person?

Water-based people consult their hearts as a guide to what is true. However, the second strongest element influences character too. The water-fire dominant are fiery romantics who sometimes express raw emotions unfiltered by thought. Those of water-earth dominance are emotional about nature, often craving the outdoors. The water-air types are the most analytical and will take a moment to reflect upon their emotions so as to express them in ways appropriate to the listener. Those of water-space can read the atmosphere in a place like a book; see people in terms of their genuine or higher selves; and are less likely to verbalize their feelings than to display them, sometimes unwittingly.

⋆ JOURNEY 3 ⋆

Do you think your character is strongly influenced by water? Determining this can be a little tricky. Being highly sensitive and living in a world that represses emotions, water-based people are seldom cavalier about their big hearts but seek to protect them by being reserved, especially upon first meeting them. In fact, people who appear emotionally explosive ('wearing emotions on their sleeve') are seldom water-based people. Those are often air people who control inflection, appear to have dramatic personalities but with less emotional attachment than a water-based person. Here are a few key questions that might help you consider how strongly water influences you. To introspect upon this question, review this chapter or just carefully consider the bulleted points:

★ Are you adaptable but emotionally sensitive?

★ Do feelings concern you more than thoughts?

★ Are you so authentic with your feelings, that it disturbs others on occasion?

★ In conversation, do you appeal more to hearts than minds?

★ Does compassion drive you to action?

★ Are you strongly attracted to water bodies?

For today's dated journal entry, introspect and post findings in your journal on whether or not you are water dominant. Be sure to explain the reasons for your findings. How does water explain or not explain many of your dominant characteristics? If water is not your strongest element but a weaker one, explain that in your journal. If you are developing an idea of your second strongest element, include that too in your analysis.

CHAPTER FOUR

ARE YOU FIRE-DOMINANT?

Acting in unhesitating and resolute ways, fire dominant people have charisma sufficient to mobilize crowds. Extroverted and strong willed, and with an aura that glows like fire, they make natural leaders. The fire-dominant feel a flame inside and want to light it in others. They have an innate sense of belonging to a world larger than themselves, sometimes making them loyal to community, tribe, clan, country or nation. That trait can find affinity with water-based people who tend to be loyal as well.

What are Some Characteristics of Fire-Dominant People?

With fire in their voice and unhesitating speech, many of our fire-based friends become 'warriors' for important causes. When alarm bells ring, they are first on the scene of trouble, rushing in like a hero, savior, or champion. They also warn of dangers to come and are the first to say, "do something before it is too late!"

Being charismatic, the fire-dominant can become actors, wonderful story-tellers and public speakers. Like those of heart, they are authentic, seldom speaking from script. They seek an audience but not to stoke their egos. Rather, they seek to inspire others with their visions, stories and ideas. When hearing their stories, you often spot them using fire as a metaphor. They might refer to the fuel, combustion and flames of a campfire to highlight their narrative.

What Kinds of Challenges do Fire-Dominant People Face?

In terms of vulnerabilities, people of fire can get overheated, grow passionate too fast, and enter into relationships too quickly. They can end relationships just as suddenly without taking the time to work things out. The ones that make them suffer the most: complacent people lacking passion. They are fiery and want action, which seems confrontational to the more sedate earth and air types.

Fire people express themselves more exuberantly than most, which sometimes disturbs others, causing interpersonal conflict. To find calm, they can employ techniques like taking a long walk in their own loving element, the sun. If weather does not permit, they might burn candles, sage, herbs, incense or wood. Being around water people calms fire people. Alternatively, a fire person, needing to cool down, might literally jump in the sea for a swim. If their fire is too dim, they need to fuel it by breathing deeply. They might take a walk in the fresh air or go for a run.

Who is Typically Compatible with Fire-Dominant People?

The passionate nature of the fire-dominant is a characteristic that works for some but not for others. Air and earth people, who like to keep a cool head, sometimes view fire people as engaging in unnecessary theatrics. The best friend of the fire person is often the soft-hearted water person who appreciates the fire person's bravery but also brings calm when there is too much drama or excitement. Fire people also make good companions and business partners for space people, as both are visionaries. So, the dreamy space person can hand their exquisite ideas to a fire person who will drive it to completion. If there is conflict between space and fire people, it owes to the space person having all the time in the world and fire person wanting action now!

What is the Ideal Environment for Fire-Dominant People?

The fire-dominant ones are often less focused on earthy things and more focused on fiery things like the sun, moon, and stars overhead. They often have homes with many windows to ensure that light (a product of fire) can enter both by day and night. They naturally seek to transform dark spaces into light-filled ones. So, if not in a naturally sunny place, you might find a home full of mirrors, crystals, skylights, candelabras and highly reflective paint!

The fire-dominant are often hospitable extroverts who entertain. Many of them have guest rooms for visiting friends and if not, they still offer the plush guest couch. They often have hearths of some kind like wood-burning stoves, fireplaces, or outdoor fire pits where they can sit under the stars at night telling stories. If you find a person with tents, sleeping bags, camper vans and gear related to road trips, it is just as likely to be a fire person as an earth person. Both, for different reasons, have a natural love of being under the stars at night.

How do the Other Elements Influence a Fire-Dominant Person?

Fire-based people usually partner up rather than work alone because, by nature, they are extroverts, inspirational leaders and visionaries. The one exception to that rule are the fire-earth types who are more grounded and can be very self-disciplined in terms of completing tasks on time without any support. Otherwise, fire people are inspired team builders who want others to join them in their endeavors. Those of fire-water dominance, being both passionate and compassionate, sway hearts easily, making them good motivational speakers. The fire-spirit types, being highly expressive in speech and manner, are good actors, charismatic and easily inspire others. Those of fire-air make great planners as they seldom overlook any detail but when it comes to delivery, they seek partners, often inspiring them with their visionary plans.

★ JOURNEY 4 ★

Is fire strong in your character or not? Do you calm yourself with fire, such as lighting candles at night? Are you enthused by the sun, stars, moon, or night sky? Do you like to lead and direct? Do you enjoy working with others? Are you fiery when emotional? Are you romantic? Do you act upon your passions? Do you love to tell tales that fire up a crowd? If you answer 'yes' to such questions, then you appear ready to explain the dominance of fire in your character. If you need to introspect more, you can review this chapter and the chart in Chapter Two.

When ready, document your findings and offer your reasons as to whether or not fire is strong in your character. If you believe fire is dominant in you, what characteristics make you fiery, more so than many others? Include your considerations on the second strongest element in your character and its influence upon your fire. If fire is not your strongest element, explain that in your journal. What makes you so sure?

CHAPTER FIVE

ARE YOU EARTH-DOMINANT?

The ones who change most dramatically from youth to maturity are the earth-dominant ones, *which is the reason* we must speak of two types. In youth, they might focus, like young guns, on the lure of the material, the shiny and visible. Emboldened by our materialistic world, they can go through a long phase of consumerism. With luck, guidance or just time, the pull of Mother Earth upon them grows stronger. Then, they flip-flop, often rejecting consumerism, materialism and competition over resources to live as part of ecosystems. That is when some earth types mature into magicians.

What are Some Characteristics of Earth-Dominant People?

Earth people are rooted in earthy matters. In fact, many of the younger earth types think that earthy matters are the only matters. We see this in posture too as they often 'stand their ground' in discussion. We even discuss them as people who seem 'very grounded'. When their down-to-earth eyes level with yours in conversation, you will see the magic power of their grounded ways. They are practical too and often good at running businesses.

Many earth people are simple of speech and sparing with words. If you meet someone so brief of speech that you want more explanation, you might be with an earth person. There are times when their straight speech is very impactful, but they are usually better observers, listeners, and actors than speakers. In fact, they often act with no spoken warning or explanation. "Why should I consult if I know what to do?"

Earth-dominant folks can change abruptly over time. Many of them, upon hearing the call of the wild, seek to escape society and its material entrapments, whether owing to social pressure, taxation or just noise. Similar to a teenager rejecting the parental home so they can make it on their own, some of our earthy types might flee the bright lights of the city to find a farm or a cabin in the woods. That movement, that inner call back to nature, that growing intolerance for the strains of materialism, often sees them evolve into more humble nature-loving beings. That call, which can occur at any age, can mark the transformation from earth person to earth magician.

What Kinds of Challenges Might Earth-Dominant People Face?

A rather widespread weakness amongst young earth people is seeing everything as material and missing out on the other elements like spirit, water, and fire. Many of them understand air (reason, rationality) but some think spiritual people are deluded, water people are too emotional and fire people are too dramatic! Those of water, fire and spirit might see this as demeaning their feelings, passions, or spirituality.

Earth people evolve into magic by knowing and loving nature. In fact, returning to Mother Nature settles nearly every issue for earth people including becoming more in touch with their own hearts, spirits and inner light (fire). As they rediscover themselves in nature, they reject the artificiality of consumerism, get along better with others, and progress toward earth magic. As their love of Mother Earth grows more spiritual, emotional and passionate, they find resonance with fire, space and heart people.

Who is Typically Compatible with the Earth-Dominant Person?

Frequently, the earth's person's best friend is an air person. Both like to maintain an even temperament (dispassionate rather than passionate) and to see the world at face value (no metaphysics). They both appreciate practical realities. However, the earth person excels more in this direction than the air person, which is sufficient to 'ground' the latter when they get too 'heady'. In return, the air-dominant ones offer the logic, rationales and ideas that help the earthy ones to succeed with projects and plans. While such partnerships are typical, each person is unique and not a stereotype. For instance, some earth-heart types are emotional and passionate, breaking with this description entirely.

What is the Ideal Environment for Earth-Dominant People?

Over time, some earth people come to reject the values of modern materialist culture to walk off the grid or leave the city for a shack in the mountains. As earth people 'discover' their need to commune with nature, they start to distance themselves from the highly socialized world. That 'call of the wild' is Mother Earth crying out to her children 'find yourselves and come home'. Many hermits are earth people.

Maturing earth types love any natural setting where there is peace, quiet and purity of elements (air, water and earth especially). They adapt to the earth whether forests, mountain, deserts or tundra. Often obsessed with good nutrition, we can find a large number of them on farms or anywhere food can be grown. They love good soils. They also speak of 'grounding themselves' with such things as a good cup of home-grown herbal tea.

Even in urban areas, it is typical to find them in simple houses made of natural materials surrounded by foliage, herb gardens, compost heaps, flowers, and tilled land. Atop and inside their cupboards are items collected from the outdoors such as plants, herbs, minerals, stones, shells, crystals, barks and leaves. Whether rural or urban, we find many earth magicians surrounded by pets, gardens, relics of nature and jars of dried herbs.

How do the Other Elements In luence an Earth-Dominant Person?

Earth people, being focused more on tangible and earthy matters than most, make great environmentalists. The exceptions are those of a strong earth-space combination who, while earthy, are also dreamers. Still, they might imagine new futures for Spaceship Earth. Those of earth-water dominance are adaptable 'go-with-the flow' types who like to work with others to achieve consensus. The earth-fire types tend to be the most passionate and are often fierce defenders of the natural world. Those of earth-air dominance, being both logical and verbal, are good with forensics or explaining any problem in detail. So, having an earth-air person on your team can ensure good planning or that appropriate action is taken.

★ JOURNEY 5 ★

Are you an earth-dominant person? Is it one of your strongest or weakest elements? Are you 'down to earth' in manner and dress? Do earthy matters preoccupy you more than others? Perhaps you think earthy matters are the only matters; then you are earth! Today, please make a journal entry describing whether you are earth-dominant or not. Include the reasons for your answers.

If you are certain of being predominately earth, please include a description of your second strongest element and its influence upon the first in your journal. Perhaps, like me, you are not very earthy at all? Then, you will need to explain why earth is not the strongest part of your character in your dated journal entry. Those of you who are not so earthy might still find that certain aspects of your character are very earthy. For example, I do not always have my feet on the ground (weak of earth) and yet I'm quite earthy when it comes to nutrition or health matters.

CHAPTER SIX

ARE YOU AIR-DOMINANT?

Alert to the outer world and how it transmits information in sound, air-dominant folks jump ten feet high if you walk up behind them to say 'boo'. They are more sensitive to atmospheric vibrations, like sounds, words or music, than those of fire, earth, water or space. They also love a high vantage point, an aerial view, for taking in a wide perspective on life. Much like birds, they have good oversight and a good sense of direction. They are the ones who can lead lost parties out of the woods.

What are Some Characteristics of the Air-Dominant Person?

Air dominant people thrive on air, breath and words. Human sound and language are related to air passages and air people tend to be word masters. Their speech patterns are dry and matter-of-fact because they select words with precision to deliver an objective or neutral assessment of any situation in well-ordered sentences. Even with loved ones, they commiserate less and lecture more on the 'logical' solution. Their humor is dry too, often expressed as a quick-witted play on words. They avoid any impression of themselves as not being in control. If feeling unhinged, they might walk straight out the door, leaving company behind, to calm themselves in the fresh air.

Certain kinds of routine gestures that air people make can help you identify them instantly. The most revealing one is the tendency to flick a hand across the air in a dismissive manner when others get too emotional or imaginative, as if to say emotions (hysteria to them) are not worth discussing! That movement of hands across the air while making their points is so typical of an air person that it might indicate 90% of them!

What Kinds of Challenges do Air-Dominant People Face?

Air-dominant people can think and analyze too much, making them overly critical, even paranoid. They like to keep all matters well-ordered and unexpected visits, or sudden changes can disturb them. Being very measured in all ways, they prefer to keep appointment books and schedule activities. So, our air-dominant friends can snap when such arrangements are disturbed. Abrupt sounds and misspoken words also see them react like a deer caught in the headlights of a car!

With a tendency toward being verbal, intellectual and orderly, air people hate chaos and can get agitated when that occurs. They are often attracted to earthy people who can calm or 'ground' their air-based friends. Other ways to bring the air-based ones into balance include worshipping the elements in daily rituals and physical exercise like running, walking or the gym. Many early risers that you see walking briskly in the open air are often air dominant ones. Music is a pretty sure bet for calming them down too. Drumming can be therapeutic as music appeals to them but also invokes (brings in) more earth, heart and spirit to quell any agitation from over-thinking.

Who is Typically Compatible with Air-Dominant People?

Air and earth people tend to relate well to each other as both like to keep a cool head. The air-based ones, being articulate, love to pontificate while the earth person tends to listen for a long while and then offer some down-to-earth words on the appropriate actions to take. Partnerships between air and earth people tend to bring calm to both.

The emotional neutrality of many air people registers best with earthy types. Those strong of fire, heart or spirit might read air people as lofty, insincere or cold. To compensate, many air people develop an extraordinarily polished and polite manner. None of these descriptions are uniformly true but point to strong tendencies. For example, air-heart people are more in touch with feelings, verbalizing what they feel sufficiently well to resonate with heart-based people.

What is the Ideal Environment for Air-Dominant Person?

Wind, fresh air, views, clarity and high places attract the air-dominant ones. You might find their homes on mountain tops, high up in skyscrapers or in places with a lookout. They favor two-story or even three-story houses. They love to stare out from high places looking for ways to piece that jigsaw puzzle of life together. Loving air, they seek to have it move freely throughout the spaces that they occupy.

How do the Other Elements Influence an Air-Dominant Person?

People of an air-fire combination are action-orientated, often using witty speech and well-reasoned ideas to inspire others ('fire' them up). People of air-water dominance love to influence hearts as well as minds and are more empathetic than the others and do not have the typical air person's 'cut and dried' ways. The air-space types, always seeking the big picture, will seek to inspire others with their big ideas. Those of air-earth dominance make good scientists and often come up with formulaic understandings that 'model' reality.

✫ JOURNEY 6 ✫

Do you think that air is strong within your character or not? Do you feel like a realist or a thinker who looks at matters most rationally? Are your decisions based upon studied information? Before taking any major step, do you like to take a deep breath and reflect upon it first? Do you love logically ordered facts? Do you expect others to adjust their views when presented with well-reasoned arguments? Are you more practical than sentimental or emotional? Do you have a good sense of direction? If you answered yes to all those questions, you are likely to be air. Just bear in mind that everyone is composed of five elements, but some elements are stronger within us than others.

Please make a written case in your journal, with evidence, as to whether or not you can be described as air dominant. If you are air, include a description of your second strongest element and its influence upon the first as today's entry in your magic journal. If not, explain why air is lower ordered in your elemental mix. Look at the reasons why air is not strong with you.

CHAPTER 7

ARE YOU SPACE OR SPIRIT-DOMINANT?

You must choose the term that suits you better but either 'space' or 'spirit' denotes a far-seeing person who imagines, plans, and envisions a better future. They think so big that we often see our space/spirit friends staring upward into space full of wonder. Yet one person sees God or a living intelligence and calls that spirit while another sees the fabric of universe, space, the most extensive of the five living elements. Your perspectives and beliefs determine which term you will employ. I generally defer to 'spirit' but am comfortable with either term as I think they both point in the same direction: something connects us all.

What Distinguishes the Spirit-Dominant Person?

Spirit people love to spark imaginations. They so love the 'big picture' that they focus on that first before considering any details. In fact, upon understanding the bigger picture, many of them leave the 'minutiae' for others to work out. Everyone should know what to do once they get the big picture! Similar to the fire-dominant, who rise like a phoenix from the ashes to reinvent themselves anew, the spirit-dominant reinvent themselves too but by employing fresh new imaginings. They evolve into their vision of self and for that reason are great philosophers, metaphysicians and magicians. They are dreamers and thinkers who create, write or invent something new. If choosing between wealth or free time to create, the spirit-dominant often choose the latter.

What Kinds of Challenges do Spirit-Dominant People Face?

For every strong point of character, there is a weaker flipside. For instance, the person of spirit engages ideas, theories and imagination beautifully but can become overly imaginative to the point of being paranoid. Sometimes they are deemed overly philosophical or too absent minded. They so love the realm of big ideas that they get called 'spacey' for failing to relate to what is happening on the ground. Think of absent-minded professors who get so wrapped up in ideas and mental machinations while walking along, that they forget where they are going! Not all spirit people are spacey but many of them disconnect from the day-to-day minutiae to face the accusation that their heads are in the clouds.

The cure for being spacey: come down to earth! Art can help bridge that gap between imagination and tangible form. Other techniques include physical therapy: mud baths, steam baths, a massage with herbal oils, a hike, a dance or anything earthy that can help 'ground' these imaginative people. Sometimes the spirit person gets anxious simply because they have no time to dream or connect with the heavens. In that case, leave them alone under the stars. Spirit people, unlike many others, might use all their leisure time for one task: letting their imaginations roam freely.

Who is Typically Compatible with Spirit-Dominant People?

Most spirit people are quite happy with themselves and seek time alone in great measure. They want to be free to explore their spirit and imagination, which seemingly knows no limits. The ones that understand that best might be people of water who, like them, are not caught up in material ambitions. They both treasure many things that are not material: emotion, passion, compassion, bold imaginings and the spirit of life. Water people bring calm to their spirit/space friends by assuring them that these are worthy values.

That the strong of spirit often dwell in the realm of the imagination can irritate earth or air people looking to ground themselves in facts, logic or practical realities. Likewise, earth and air people can irritate people of spirit by being too materialistic and narrow minded. To a spirit person, the atmosphere in a room is far more important than the material things in it. The spilt drink on the floor or coffee table is much less important to them than comradery or high spirits, which can lead to conflict with earth or air types who might get very agitated about any physical mess!

What is the Ideal Environment for the Spirit Person?

Loving the imagination, spirit-dominant people settle in whatever environment allows them much leisure time to be alone and at peace. Loving the starry heavens, many seek such a view from their homes. Most tend to be rather minimalist in terms of furnishings or earthy belongings. You might find them in spaces free of any clutter, ornaments or furnishings that 'trap' them into dealing with the material. There are exceptions, however, as some spirit-earth people, being both lofty and grounded, become artists. You might find these types with a particular studio or a workshop full of tools for their self-expression.

How do the Other Elements Influence the Spirit-Dominant Person?

The character of the spirit person is strongly influenced by the element that is secondarily dominant. *Spirit-fire* people are big picture types who are both imaginative and dramatic in presenting ideas but, typically, are not much interested in implementation. Those of *spirit-water* have an unhesitating emotional honesty that tends to stir hearts into action, but they also tend be less involved in delivery. Those of *spirit-air* dominance are like architects who know how to design, sell their ideas and lay out all the facts when sharing their designs but are not so interested in any physical labor. It is mainly the *spirit-earth* types who bridge that gap between design and reality to land themselves on the ground as leaders. A good partnership between spirit-air and spirt-earth types can help to ensure good planning and delivery on the ground.

⋆ JOURNEY 7 ⋆

Is spirit (or space if you prefer) strong in your character or not? Do you feel that the spirit in a room is more important than the material items in it? If people are laughing and happy and suddenly brought down by negativity, are you upset? Do you download information from the universe like some people download data off a computer? Do you like to dream big? Do you see knowledge as temporary and in flux? Do you feel strongly connected to the Cosmos? Are you so imaginative that you crave time for the imagination alone? Have you ever entered so deeply into reflection that you missed a bus or an appointment? Are you creative? Do you delight in the stars? If you answered yes to most of those questions, you are probably spirit/space.

Please make a written case in your journal, with evidence, as to whether or not you can be described as dominant of spirit (or use the word space if that makes you more comfortable). Try to identify your second strongest element as well. If not strongly spirit, explain why spirit has a weaker influence on your character than other elements. Look for reasons why spirit is not strong with you.

CHAPTER EIGHT

DOCUMENT YOUR ELEMENTAL MIX

This chapter concludes our overview of how to use the elements to describe your character. Can you now describe your entire character in terms of the five elements? That is today's journey where we connect the dots between your character strengths and weaknesses.

Why Would Anyone Highlight and Describe their Weaknesses?

Most people repress or ignore their weaknesses and highlight their strengths. That undermines their magic because there are times when knowing your weaknesses is a major source of power. You might be silent when appropriate or find compassion for another who shares your fallibilities (empathy). When you know both your strong and weak points of character, rather than your strengths only, you become humble, which is a superpower, making you more attuned to the world around you. Knowing both your strengths and weaknesses and how they correspond *strengthens* your magic.

Have you ever played the family game called 'rock, paper, scissors'? There are variations on the rules but basically two players gesture one of three hand positions at the same time on a count of three. If I display scissors (two fingers extended) and you display rock (a solid fist), you blunt me, but had I displayed paper (a flat hand), I cover the rock and win. Scissors cut paper but paper covers stone and rock blunts scissors. You see, the strength or weakness of each item is relational rather than absolute. Everything in the universe, including we humans, have both strengths and weaknesses that correspond. It is useful to chart that, which will be the journey further below.

If you think about it, the weakest people are those who claim to have no weaknesses. The strong laugh at their weaknesses. Magicians seldom reject their 'shadow' side but embrace it so that it transmutes into a source of power. Those not acknowledging human weaknesses are defensive and that defensiveness can rack up more troubles than the weaknesses themselves. Rather, bring light and dark into balance than hide or eliminate one or the other.

Can I Describe my Strengths and Weaknesses Together?

Yes. That is today's journey. Further below, you will chart how your strengths and weaknesses correspond. Charting it out (strengths in one column, weaknesses in another) and thinking about it will help you to choose your activities wisely, ask for help when needed, lead when warranted, retreat when it is wise, reduce negativity and harmonize with Mother Nature, all of which are critical to magic. For instance, if we never review our disrespect for Mother Earth (a weakness in humanity) and how that came about, we will never correct a behavior, most unmagical, that is killing life on our planet.

Pretending to be full of light all of the time is like speeding down a busy roadway at night with your headlights on high beam. It is more likely to cause accidents than to showcase your enlightenment. Humans are never free of all blind spots and challenges, but magic offers a way to address them. We can routinely rebalance the elemental energies both within and without our being. Doing so brings healing, joy, and light into ourselves and others. It seems obvious to me that we must balance the strong and weak sides of our characters to live in harmony with nature, a value held by most magicians.

Are you Saying Positive Thinking can be Detrimental to our Planet?

Science would collapse if its practitioners simply chucked all phenomena into two bins labeled positive or negative. Magic is the same. Boxing yourself as either positive or negative does not account for the alchemy of dark and light within your being. It leaves you in a black and white universe with no shades of grey. A preconditioned response, either positive or negative, to all phenomena on earth is ridiculous, as life is nuanced and requires responses appropriate to changing circumstances.

Since your character is the primary source of your magic, those who repress their true selves to 'be positive' are not magical by virtue of not expressing their full character. Magic is in our nature but to find it we must embrace all sides of our characters. To be blind to our weaknesses only leaves us vulnerable to manipulation, depression, inappropriate behavior and disease. Of course, people commonly repress their weaker side. Perhaps they fear abuse, hate, violence, gossip or character assassination, but whatever we repress in ourselves becomes the subconscious shadow-side of our characters, which can burst like a dam and often under inappropriate circumstances, which is not magical.

Can I Make Accurate Observations About Myself?

The human brain seems to have an 'objective' setting where we can dispassionately examine our strengths and weaknesses together without adding prejudices or emotional baggage. That kind of 'dispassion' helps us to know and express ourselves better and therefore act appropriately. Are we not more sensitive to someone holding the same failings as ourselves? Do we not understand them better when we see the same weakness in ourselves?

Surely, you have certain behavioral and cognitive tendencies, which can be improved, changed, corrected or addressed? Can you look dispassionately at yourself, without judgment? If you can, it offers a path to magic along with inner peace and making peace with others. It becomes easier to handle many of life's issues when we see both our strong and weak points of character. It is within you to do that on today's journey as you issue a final statement on your elemental mix.

★ JOURNEY 8 ★

On today's journey (below) you will look at both your character weakness and strengths dispassionately, just to help you understand them better. Of course, we are not just talking heads and we have feelings, but we can contain them for a bit of analysis. Just re-center yourself in the heart afterwards.

Please write an evidence-based and neutral description of your entire elemental composition. Make use of the elements to describe:

★ Your strengths and weaknesses as a character

★ How your weaknesses and strengths correspond

★ An example of how your weaknesses sometimes turn to strengths

★ An example of how your strengths sometimes turn to weaknesses

Support your statements, making use of all evidence gathered in these processes. Consider sketches, photos or illustrations where applicable. A chart illustrating your strengths on one side and corresponding weakness on the other might be helpful.

Depending on your experience, the questions bulleted below might be relevant to formulating/stimulating a reply. So, before starting on your entry, just review these:

★ Did you find two equally strong elements and three weaker ones? That is a common pattern. If so, how does the interplay of the two stronger elements play out in your character?

★ How do the weaker elements (usually three) describe your character (negatively and positively)? Do you understand the reasons why some elements were seen as subordinate to others in your character?

★ Do you feel that you are dominated by one strong element followed by four weaker ones? That is also fairly common

★ Do you have three equally strong elements and two weaker ones? While that is rare, it does occur

★ Did you find you had five equally strong elements? That is so unusual that it indicates a need to review these chapters again. It is the balance of strengths and weaknesses that give people character. It is important to give equal consideration to your character weaknesses, which people seldom do but is most empowering

The remaining chapters will either reinforce your findings or challenge them. If challenged, just return to refine this journal entry later. A magic journal is a living document that we constantly review to improve practice.

CHAPTER 9

EXAMINE YOUR ASSUMPTIONS

Assumptions are prefabricated views of reality that blind us to the moment including what is authentic about ourselves, other people, or situations. We find some stale explanation or fixed idea that we never considered properly and pin it, like a label, onto the present. Instead of immersing ourselves in the moment, we fit what we see into our pre-existing prejudices, socialization, indoctrination, silly whims, fantasies, ideologies or neuroses.

How do Assumptions Undermine Magic?

We empower ourselves in magic through presence, awareness, and spontaneity. We find our magic spark in the moment. If we do not leave all assumptions behind, we are blinded to who or what is before us right now. Whenever we drag the past into the present, we kill spontaneity and therefore magic. Judging someone's life is full of assumptions and so it kills magic. Instead of employing empathy and compassion to understand another properly, we slap them with a label, killing the magic moment.

Assumptions and judgments are more dangerous than most seem to think because they can be driven into the body politique and divide entire nations. Knowing the human tendency to judge and persecute, politicians seeking power often pick out certain groups for persecution so they can 'rise up' through the politics of oppression. For instance, Hitler rose to power by encouraging verbal or physical assaults on Jews, Gypsies, gays, and other non-conforming groups. So, public thinking can be engineered by the media, power hierarchies, bureaucrats and demagogues, as emerged in recent years with social media, but the degree of it and the long history of it is not fully understood by the public. It is important to look at that because living in a world of propaganda, judgments and assumptions blocks one's path to magic.

What Can I do to Reduce my Assumptions About People?

To see another clearly, we must reduce our assumptions, remove the labels, drop the stories, and find ourselves in a state of non-judgment. Most of us cannot sum up our own lives in a label or sentence and yet attempt to sum up someone else with a whole different life experience. Here are six ways that reducing assumptions and suspending judgment makes our lives more magical:

★ As magic celebrates what is unique, rather than what is conformist about each of us, it is not really possible to be a judgmental magician. By recognizing what is unique about ourselves, we not only empower ourselves but see the magic in others, making all lives more magical

★ Magic requires that we be present, while judging creates fear and anxiety over past or future events, undermining practice

★ Our assumptions and judgments alienate us from others, while suspending them increases our influence and opportunities to partner, which is magical

★ Judgment makes you hard on yourself and therefore you are hard on others, less present and less magical

★ Judgmental people, with their scowling faces, are often energetically unattractive, reducing their magical power and influence

★ Magic requires that we see the world in more holistic ways, but that is impeded by assumptions that narrow people and events to labels and judgments

How Can I Reign in these Judgments and Assumptions?

Here are twelve ways to stop making assumptions and judging everyone you meet:

★ Choose to live in a magical world full of unique characters, places and situations, so that you always see with fresh eyes, making no assumptions. Know that no two moments, no two people and no two situations are alike

★ Live more from the heart than the head. Your natural magic emerges from the unhampered and full expression of your whole-hearted being, while your head is where all the erroneous notions, propaganda and socialization are stored

★ Identify any thoughts producing fear. Then, remove them as they represent implanted ideologies and prefabricated views not originating from you, which is not magical

★ Eliminate the idea that you make a good judge of people. You cannot know more about another person than you know about yourself and it is a lifelong journey to know ourselves

★ Choose to be in a continual state of non-judgment. It will enhance or advance your magical abilities including accurately assessing situations, communicating clearly, and resolving conflict

★ Assume less and ask more questions to avoid erroneous judgments

★ Simply move away from people that make you feel uncomfortable, without adding a judgment

★ Rather than blaming others for what you feel, own your feelings and share them in an authentic and calm manner

★ Observe yourself judging. The more you observe yourself making judgments (become conscious), the less likely you are to continue the practice

★ Immerse yourself in the moment, rather than destroying it with your grudges, prejudices and stale ideas

★ Quit judging yourself or feeling guilty, as such behaviors make you more likely to judge others

★ Treat others as you would have them treat you (egalitarianism)

★ JOURNEY 9 ★

This is an easy journey but has four parts. First, take a seat and try to identify five beliefs, fears or ideas about yourself or the world that are actually assumptions. Perhaps, these were instilled in you from birth for the purposes of mass social control or just bad ideas you took from random experiences (e.g. I cannot sing; I am not smart; life is a competition). Then, jot these down, one each, on five slips of paper. Each slip represents a characteristic thought or behavior that might be negating your true character and therefore your magic.

Second, recall the character of the natural person that you were as a child before too much indoctrination. If you cannot remember, perhaps ask some relatives to stimulate your understanding. Afterward, jot down on five slips of paper five magical characteristics (one per slip) that you had in youth that you fear might have disappeared or weakened (e.g. a belief in magic; trust in the universe; expressive and free spirited).

Third, grab a match and set up a ceremony of fire for those negative beliefs that might be suppressing your true character. One-by-one, burn each slip to the incantation: "It is me who shapes my future." For each slip, say it seven times with such conviction that you can let your socialization go.

Fourth, assemble the remaining five slips of paper covering character traits that you had in early youth that disappeared under socialization. Repeat this out loud seven times, "I was born and remain a unique expression of the cosmos." Paste these slips into your journal. Afterward, list and describe each of these five natural character traits. Explain how they can help you unleash your own brand of magic.

CHAPTER 10

DEFINE YOUR VALUES

The main source of power in practical magic is your character but values shape character. So, today's journey will have you introspect and review the values that befit your character. To stimulate that inward journey, let me provide an example of how to introspect and define your own values by sharing four values pertinent to my practice:

★ Worshipping nature

★ Finding harmony in diversity

★ Embracing humility

★ Speaking from the heart

As I review the values bulleted above, do not assume any of them to be yours. You do not have to adopt my values at all. If these values match yours, include them in your practice, but the aim of today's journey (further below) is to have you introspect and define *your* highest values.

Should I Worship Nature?

While you need not practice my way or see the world as I do, thinking in such a manner led to the magic that I practice. I plugged into the web of life, listened, observed, and affirmed my unity with nature, a higher self and a divine intelligence. I suspect that is how magic evolved for early humans, too, as they tried to make sense of their world.

I would recommend that you worship nature as a path to magic. To value nature to the point of worshipping her shifts one's focus and behavior toward promoting harmony, reversing widespread environmental destruction, cooperating and sharing. Through worship, I moved away from a narrow concept of self, based on ego, to a cosmic outlook based on ethos and harmony. For instance, the more I commune (e.g. worship, pray, meditate) with nature, the less separate I feel and the more I start to psychically upload or download information from her. I see the worship of nature as becoming part of her, which ushers in magic gifts.

Of course, worshipping nature does not make your practice like mine. You might climb mountains or swim in the sea. I commune with nature wherever I find her in my daily life, which is everywhere! It includes my partner, my dog Sandy, the flowers and insects in my garden and the entire earth, atmosphere, sun and stars around me. You can connect to nature from a prison cell! So, being with nature does not require that you climb mountains. Rather, you need to construct a practice that includes you as part of nature. You can achieve that through worship or by communing with nature.

Did You Say I Can Find Harmony in Diversity?

Yes. I worship Mother Nature and know that it is diversity, variation amongst and between species, which enables adaptation to change. Since we are at the top of the food chain, destroying nature's biodiversity destroys the mechanism by which humans adapt to change. Our abuse of the earth for profit is making environments increasingly similar all over the world, reducing diversity, which threatens the survival of many species including humans.

From my perspective, we need to value nature more. Most people seem to see money as the source of wealth, rather than nature, which makes people exploit nature for profit right to the point of human-induced species extinction. For example, we clear-cut rainforests for monoculture crops, like palm oil, which are destroying hundreds of thousands of species of co-dependent plants and animals. We have killed so much that we might never really account for all the damage, to things like soil, good nutrition, climate and culture (e.g. rainforest peoples are removed).

When I look at human uniformity advancing to the point of killing nature and culture, I realize we need to break this spell: nature is just another commodity for sale. If we saw nature as a creative living intelligence or the source of wealth, rather than money, we could greatly slow the speed of human induced species extinction. So, I place a high value on finding harmony through diversity.

How is Being Humble of Value to your Magic Practice?

Can a magician be an arrogant, egotistical, vain, greedy, competitive, inconsiderate, or ungraceful individual living in a world of assumptions? I think magic takes place when we are non-judgmental, considerate, forgiving, ethical, ecological, promoting harmony, gracious, finding common ground and helping others with no expectation of remuneration. We can sum up that set of values in the concept of humility, a characteristic I find *essential* to being a good magician. Why? Humility puts a halt to assumptions, allowing you to see clearly. The highest form of the magician's art might be evocation such as contacting fairies, spirits, elementals, departed ancestors and other beings in adjacent dimensions but in my experience, people who think that other forms of life exist only to satisfy human wishes, whims and desires, spoil such contact. It fails. In fact, it *requires* humility to accept that there might be equally intelligent entities, even more advanced ones, that escape our attention.

How Can Speaking from the Heart have Magical Values?

The heart refers to what we feel deep inside, which has magical values. If I communicate heart-to-heart, I am freer, more expressive, and more authentic. Saying what I feel is non-manipulative but telling you what to think is manipulative. When I speak direct from my heart to you, my words resonate with authenticity (being true to myself). I can accurately state what I feel, which is being authentic, while my theories on reality might not be accurate at all.

Is the heart, then, a magical source of truth? I would say yes. A lie detector test does not measure the brain for truth but pulse, heart rate and blood pressure. So, the detector is partly based on the concept that the heart cannot lie. It catches the contradiction between what someone says and feels. The heart's blood vessels, that are in every part of our body including our faces, can involuntarily 'flush' when we lie. Thus, the heart leads us to the truth. Living and speaking from the heart regularly can help you to deprogram from the indoctrination and false beliefs that block the path to magic.

When we value heart-to-heart communication, we see empathy increase and our communication with others improve. By contrast,

58

people who take sides in 'objective' and 'intellectual' arguments often end up fighting as they take up opposed ideological positions requiring some form of accounting. Who is right? The victor gets an ego boost. Yet, if communicating well and expressing feelings in real time, do we even need ideologies or to convince others that we are right? By owning and expressing more feelings, we take responsibility for what we feel and are not telling others how they should live, which reduces divisions, nurtures peace and enables magical values.

★ JOURNEY 10 ★

Can you now define your values independent of me? Reflect upon your life and character to identify at least five values that are priorities for you. If any values of mine (from the narrative above) matched yours, you can include them but if you do a good job, you will specify a combination of values that are specific to your unique character. Once you identify your values, you are more in touch with who you are, which is part of the journey to discover magic.

List the five values (more if you wish) in your magic journal, possibly in priority order (if feasible). Then, describe and explain each value in the manner given in the chapter (a paragraph or two on each). Be sure to date your journal entry.

CHAPTER 11

PROSPER THROUGH GRACIOUSNESS

Worshipping money more than love or life, the human condition, is killing nature. Humans, for their own survival, must learn to live in harmony with each other and nature. Thus, we need to redefine prosperity. How can we do that? We need to be more gracious. We can give to each other out of love for having experienced love. Communities that live that way are in a state of grace: full of love, appreciation, caring, sharing and other ways natural to being human. To experience that state of grace is to experience prosperity. If you give out of expectation of a reward, your humanity is gone and graciousness as a currency is smashed.

Do you Think People are not Defining Prosperity Accurately?

Correct. Many people today define prosperity as competing with their neighbors for material things (rather than sharing) and worshipping money above nature. We care so little about nature and so much about money that we exploit everyone and everything around us, which is not graceful at all. Would it not be far more gracious to treat wealth as reverence for each other and all life? That definition includes the concept of stewardship. Instead of competing, we could cooperate during our lifetimes to maintain the gifts of the earth for future generations.

What does Graciousness have to do with Prosperity?

Grace takes many forms such as gratitude, humility, reverence, spiritual wisdom, acknowledgement, generosity, kindness and love. Graciousness stands in opposition to greed, hording and competition over resources, as such behaviors show no respect for the interdependency of life. 'We are one' might be the motto for grace. It is the precondition for living harmoniously with Mother Earth and all other species on the planet, which is real prosperity.

Can you Give me an Example of Being Graceful?

Before the great conquests, tribal peoples around the world normally defined wealth as time available to commune with each other and nature, which is graciousness. In fact, the tribal structure in pre-conquest times was normally communal (rather than competitive) and gracious since members shared tasks to produce leisure for the *entire tribe*. Many tribal peoples, globally, had magic ceremonies dedicated to the sun, moon, stars, birds, animals, or any part of their lives for which they were grateful. Stewardship, a responsibility to maintain the abundance and beauty of nature for future generations, was part of most tribal belief systems in the Americas before the conquests. I think that graciousness owed to not being monetized or seeing wealth as nature.

What does Grace Have to do with Magic?

How can we progress with magic if we just want to take and give nothing back? How can we live in harmony with both nature and others, if we want to exploit them both for personal gain? Graciousness is about recognizing your role as a steward of the earth. An individual who does not appreciate the earth is not qualified to build the movement to conserve it. It requires grace to cooperate, share insights and solve problems together and that is why grace is *the* magical way to be.

What Stops us from Being Graceful?

We need to break the spell that *nature is a commodity that we can strip for personal wealth and power.* We need to embrace the magical view that nature is a living intelligence worthy of worship. Then, we are less likely to assault our mother for economic gain. So, respecting nature as our mother would help move us from destroying life on this planet to nature worship or stewardship, which are signs of being graceful. You will see that graciousness can magically transform your world on today's journey.

★ JOURNEY 11 ★

I want you to observe how an act of graciousness contributes to prosperity by contributing something to the neighborhood. First, explore your neighborhood. First, take your journal along with either a map or photo device (like your phone), and go explore your neighbourhood. Your mission: scout out the nearest public place that has been de-natured in some way, large or small. You might take note of a neighborhood park or vacant field that has been neglected. Identify a place where you can help restore nature in some tangible way that does not take too long. Take photographs, sketches, or notes.

While inspecting the neighborhood, practice graciousness with those whom you meet. Share kind words, any neighborhood concerns, and document any learning from such conversations. Ask them about neighborhood concerns. Discuss how you would address any issues or concerns that neighbors have about the environment. If you cannot find someone around the neighborhood, make a phone call to a neighbor or friend so that issues are identified.

Once you have identified an issue, decide what actions you can take, however modest, to help the whole neighborhood. Must you write or call the council? Would you canvass neighbors? Could you simply repair something or help restore a neglected garden? Enter your plans in your journal and include a time budget and a list of available tools needed.

Now, devote some available time to breathing life back into a deteriorated public space. Otherwise, solve some neighborhood issue or contribute to its resolution. Do not overdo this. You want to demonstrate, in a small way, that graciousness, a powerful factor in magic, can make a huge difference to public life. Take before-and-after photos or else use drawing, sketches or illustrations of some kind.

Describe in your journal, with illustrations, what you accomplished including how you identified the problem, how much time it took, what was involved, who was involved, and the outcome. Then, find a way to share that journey with neighbors. Very often, others join us in gifting a better world once we start. So, be sure to monitor the social impact of your activity, as well, and describe it in your journal. You might start a movement!

CHAPTER 12

THINK COSMIC

Very few people think, let alone act, at a cosmic (universal) scale. Yet those who did, like Jesus or Buddha, are worshipped by many because they expressed an unusually high level of awareness. We call it a *cosmic consciousness* when we evolve beyond our narrow self-interests to see we are the world. If we can learn to think cosmically, in terms of what is best for *all* living things, we can restore harmony to our planet. Thinking in narrow and selfish ways explains why we are seeing the destruction of plants, animals, oceans, rivers, cultures, peoples, climate and ecosystems. We can help reverse that by thinking cosmic, which is a magical superpower.

How do I Lift my Consciousness to a Cosmic Level?

Few have sustained a cosmic consciousness for long periods. However, communing with nature, God or the Cosmos through daily worship (e.g. prayer, mediation, or ritual) lifts one's consciousness to a higher level than it would otherwise be. Regular worship (communing with nature) helps me to drop the ego and focus, with gratitude, on something bigger than myself (like God or the living Cosmos), which immediately dispels any depression or negativity too. Many of us start with discipline (schedule a time for this routine) but eventually the sheer joy of communion makes worship regular. The degree to which you are thinking cosmic can be measured by how much joy you feel.

What is the Value of Thinking Cosmic?

Thinking cosmic teaches us about the natural order of the universe. We learn of natural laws because we look wider, beyond our wants and desires, to observe all of nature and consider our relationship to it.

Our outlook then shifts to considering the needs of nature rather than just ourselves. Upon learning that nature is alive, an intelligent energy of which we are a part, we grow more joyous. By contrast, when we separate ourselves from nature, we speak of conquering and exploiting her instead of protecting her. Our focus narrows from the common good to competitive self-interest.

Are you Saying we Should Live Closer to Nature?

Yes. We must live much closer to the earth to develop sustainable ways of life. Most tribal peoples, before the advent of massive states, saw themselves as blessed by earth's gifts and wanted to maintain the bounty for future generations. We lost that sense of stewardship in a history of conquests. We then took a conquering approach to nature and now treat the earth like a resource warehouse. That exploitative and conquering culture must change, or many species and a good percentage of humanity will not survive. We must live closer to nature so that we can understand and protect her much better. She gives us life, but we are killing her.

Does Conformity Destroy Nature?

Conformity, the historic product of tyrants seeking power over the masses, destroys culture, which is about small groups of humans adapting to nature. If we have culture, people create ways of life appropriate to each ecosystem, which we call adaptation. We have tremendous natural variation upon the earth, and the role of human culture is to adapt to this variation.

Now, if everyone is alike, predictable and controllable, we start to kill culture, natural diversity and adaptation. The will to homogenize owes to a history of conquest and culture killing (genocide, ethnocide). Both during conquest and hundreds of years into its aftermath, we feel tremendous pressures to appease a small group of rulers or elites rather than adapt to our natural surroundings. Most of us give in to these tremendous pressures. Historically, we have been thrown off the land, seen stewardship destroyed, watched genocide kill our cultures and watched our kids programmed through school and mass media. The pressures are so enormous that most give in, but it dulls our magic light by killing culture, truth, and the will to resist someone else's agenda. We give up our magic for servitude.

The 'masses' are people historically forced to give up land, culture, magic and community to conform to a system of class divisions, competitive behavior, and wage labor. Over a long 10,000-year history, people were forced off the land to create a hierarchical system that would concentrate power and wealth in fewer and fewer hands. In the recent Ages of Colonialism and Neocolonialism (15th to 21st centuries), we shifted from tribe, culture and place to the modern state system. Magical peoples (indigenous peoples) were removed, lines drawn, and culture destroyed to steepen the hierarchy. Now, we are in a situation where very few people make decisions affecting billions of people and thousands of ecosystems. While this top-heavy system is supported by armies, police, ideology, propaganda, flags and songs, it is not stable. One wrong decision in say, Washington or Beijing, can spell catastrophe for the entire world.

Power hierarchies held together by submission and conformity destroy the human spirit, so much so that people at the bottom of the hierarchy tend to oppress each other. Like victims in Nazi concentration camps, deprived of spirit, they regulate each other. How can we intervene to stop this oppression? A magical way is to lift our consciousness from self-interest to cosmic. By thinking less selfishly and more globally, we can promote a more egalitarian and harmonious way of life. When we see nature as us, we start to restore it and to create more harmonious and egalitarian relations with our fellow beings, both human and non-human. Anyone thinking cosmic helps to move us from being ego-based (competitive) to being ethos-based (cooperative) so that the decisions we make restore our environments rather than further damage them through violent exploitation.

How does one Learn to Think Cosmic?

We replace self-centered thinking with a consciousness of the whole. We expand our consciousness from 'me' to seeing and acting in concert with nature, a very large all-knowing intelligence of which we are a part. Guidance from that intelligence comes from communion with it. Regular communion jettisons egocentric thinking, ambition, greed, competition, jealousy, lust for power and other dark feelings and behaviors. The longer we commune with nature, the more our awareness expands. Some meditate to find that union. Some dance to the sun to invoke light into themselves, which they later share as joy or love. Let's find a way for you to expand your consciousness to cosmic on today's journey.

★ JOURNEY 12 ★

Having greater awareness of the whole is what we seek to achieve with a cosmic consciousness. Since it requires practice, I would describe it as a discipline, but to a greater degree, it is about seeking joy. Connecting to the intelligence behind all intelligence brings a tremendous sense of well-being. It reminds you that you are part of nature, part of a universal intelligence, which lifts the spirit.

So, with joy in mind, can you find your way to a cosmic consciousness, even if only for short periods? Could you spend some time in communion (anywhere from 10 to 60 minutes) with this grand intelligence and capture that experience in your journal? You are part of this intelligence and can connect today. Identify a place and a way to commune with the great universal intelligence of which you are a part.

The objective of communing with nature is to so lift your spirit that you feel at one with the universe. Start by choosing how to connect. Do you choose dance? Meditation? A walk? A swim in the sea? Drawing? Writing? Singing? Playing a harp? Observing nature? Choose whatever means lifts your soul. Look for the method that brings you the highest level of joy. What unleashes your joy when communing with this great universe? How can you make your best connection with an intelligent Cosmos?

Now choose a place that suits you. Follow your inner joy. You might wander up a mountain and take much inspiration from quietly looking out over a majestic scene (consciousness-raising). Some do nothing more extraordinary than pray every night at bedtime, which also sees one's awareness expand. Others might dance under sunny skies or sit quietly by the sea contemplating the roll of the waves. I might sit quietly outside at night inspecting the vastness of the stars overhead and see my awareness expanding as I connect more deeply to the elements swirling around me.

In a dated journal entry, describe your experience of a cosmic consciousness. What did you do? What did you achieve? What confluence of factors produced a moment or a series of them whereby you really felt at one with the universe? What, if anything, was problematic? Did you experience a joyful kind of upliftment? Describe what you did to commune and its impact on lifting your consciousness to cosmic. Include photographs, drawing or illustrations as relevant.

★ PART TWO ★

SOME TOOLS OF PRACTICE

Before we reach Section Three and start designing rituals, I want to ensure that every reader has access to a toolbox of practices. So, Part Two is a practical section that reviews various tools that you can use when designing rituals in Section Three. We will start with herbs and botanicals. Learn about these tools and complete the journeys but in Section Three, you can leave behind any tools that do not appeal to you. You are not restricted to these tools either but might have to do some research for Section Three if few of the Section Two tools appeal to you (unlikely). These are common tools of practice, most of which I use daily.

CHAPTER 13

MAKE USE OF HERBS AND BOTANICALS

The term 'herb' refers to particular plants or parts thereof, while 'botanical' is a broader term for all mixes of herbs and plants including elixirs, potions and sachets. The homes of many magicians, particularly earth magicians, are often full of herbs and botanicals for healing, protection, purification, mood-lifting, spells, ceremonies, potions, cleansing, luck and transformation.

The Best Way to Learn About Herbs and Botanicals

An experienced earth magician might tell you much about herbs and botanicals. Holistic health practitioners can tell you a lot too. You can find books and websites that explain the magic of herbs and botanicals. Traditional peoples, the intact indigenous populations amongst us, can tell you much about them too. Yet there might be no greater teacher than personal experimentation wherein you learn about herbs, plants and natural medicines while developing potions to resolve your own issues. A focus on self-healing offers:

★ A practical way to learn about herbs or mixtures

★ Tells you which ones are quickly available

★ Prevents you from be overwhelmed by 'general information' on this subject, which is massive

If I wrote one page for every form of herb and botanical (e.g. fresh plants, dried herbs, infusions, extracts, oils, scents, incense and sachets, etc.) I could easily create a volume of 350,000 pages! So, base your investigation into herbs and botanicals upon your own needs. Then, a day will arrive, without effort, when you find yourself inspiring others with tales of your healing journeys into the magical world of herbs and botanicals.

Where to Find Herbs and Botanicals

If you look around your neighborhood, you might see many herbs that are freely available. Sometimes great herbs, like dandelion, are growing in the cracks of city sidewalks and spreading across abandoned lots and fields! Often what is treated as a weed in contemporary society, is tremendous for healing and psychic work. There is a lovely hemlock tree, quite near to me too, that it is remarkably beautiful but incredibly poisonous. So, always use available references to check out what you find.

Growing your own plants might be the easiest way to access herbs safely and they can come in planter boxes from the nursery. If your environment is not conducive to either growing or collecting herbs, research herbs that you can obtain from shops (health shops, nurseries). Make sure they promise something of value to you like curing an ailment, inducing peace or enabling a restful night. Test them out at your leisure.

Some Ways to Employ Herbs

I stock my home with herbs specific to my own health needs and those of my partner. At least three times a day I make herbal teas. I also anoint myself with oils and tinctures for cleansing and protection. I burn herbs, especially sage, at the start of indoor rituals to remove negative energy, create a harmonious space and lift my own consciousness. Certain botanical oils calm me, improve my mood, strengthen my thinking, attract good luck or positively influence others. I love to bathe in herbal potions although, being in a drought-prone environment, it is a luxury I seldom experience! On occasion, I have worn herb sachets.

Herbs that are Useful for Magic

Below I describe five magic herbs to stimulate your desire to find out more:

★ **LAVENDER:** This is one of my favorite oils to wear at night because it brings me a sense of peace, helps with sleep, attracts love, and it induces and develops psychic powers. It also has the excellent side effect of keeping mosquitoes at bay!

★ **ELDER:** This is a good one if you spend any time driving out evil spirits. For that reason, elder is popular as a wand! It can also be hung over doorways and windows

★ **FRANKINCENSE:** This is powerful for driving out evil spirits. So much so that it is commonly used in exorcism. More important for everyday purposes, it accelerates spiritual growth, heals (amazing in skin cream), improves vision, and deepens meditative states

★ **JASMINE:** Burn this as incense next to the bed at night or just wear it as an oil and you can have some amazing dreams. It can help promote abundance by making one more resourceful. Many say it aids in astral projection, although I do not use it for that

★ **THYME:** Have you ever suffered from bad dreams? Then stuff sachets of this herb into your pillow as it helps cure that problem. It is also something you can use in purification rituals. Keeping it around can increase your psychic abilities as well. It is useful for those of us in the profession of doing readings

Safety

Practical magicians employ herbs for upliftment, healing and protection but there are also some who use herbs in a counterproductive manner. So, always be wary of herbs that are presented to you. Never let botanical mixtures land in your lap that were developed to hurt, manipulate or exploit others. Always check out any collected herbs against a reference book before ingesting them!

★ JOURNEY 13 ★

Learning about herbs is fun and practical, especially if you find herbs that can address some personal issues. For instance, if you are restless at night, you might want to test out some thyme or lavender under the pillow to improve your sleep. So, today's journey is to find a book, website or source for identifying herbs in all forms (natural, scents, powders, oils, incense, etc.). Browse through it and select five herbs that might have some personal value, but you will not know until you test them out. Each of us is unique and responds differently.

Start your dated journal entry by describing the five herbs you selected and why they interested you. Then, test out each. If you make this fun (a secret to success in magic) and pace yourself, you can expand your knowledge rather quickly. You can break up the journey into five small experiments over several days. Simply test out each herb and then document your findings. What was the purpose of the herb? How did you test it out? What was the result?

This is a journey that you can take often, perhaps once or twice a week! Test out herbs from now on and integrate them into your life, starting with teas perhaps. Gradually you can develop, buy or acquire oils, potions or herbal mixtures that enhance your magic powers.

CHAPTER 14

EMIT COLORS FROM YOUR AURA

Electromagnetic devices show that humans emit waves of color and glow more than most animals. While such 'halos' of color around human heads and bodies have been reported since biblical times, we started to photograph these auras early in the 20th century with Kirlian photography. We learned that our electromagnetic light field or 'aura' comes in various hues of color, which rise and fall in intensity from day to night. Stretch out your arms perpendicular to each side and you have a fairly good estimate of the extent of your auric field. We might emit this oval shaped light up to six feet or so around our bodies by day but in sleep, it might be less extensive.

Adjusting our Electromagnetic Output

I expend much of my time absorbing light energy from the sun, moon or stars in rituals as a way of familiarizing myself with the Cosmos and finding harmony within it. I also think such practice helps me to extend my auric field. A longstanding practice amongst magicians, when sensing danger, is to issue white light, outward from one's own aura, to create a zone of safety around oneself and anyone nearby. With practice, I extended that. How do I know? I find that it helps create, at minimum, a feeling of safety for me and for those nearby me.

Learning to Control an Auric Field

Each practical magician experiments or practices with colors to see what works best. What one person calls 'blue' is not necessarily your blue. When we see color, it is really about a range of radiating frequencies along a huge continuum. Furthermore, each practitioner is radiating a different auric field. We see and experience colors differently and are affected differently. To overlook oneself as a factor in a magic practice just produces a poor practice. You are the expert on your practice and not me or any other.

The wavelengths of colors that lift my energy I find out in the sun. In other words, I try to invoke real color into my being through outdoor worship (light is the source of color). I then return home to lay still, breathing in and out the colors that I found/absorbed outside. The time in the sun appears to have an impact on my aura or electromagnetic output.

In addition to invoking sunlight, I use breathwork and visualization to employ color and issue, by that method, a zone of intense and vibrant colors around me. For instance, I have a favorite hue of pink, discovered this way, that helped me to achieve a higher state of energetic resonance. I can also breathe that color in and out until I enter a trance, a portal into the beyond. The chakra color long reputed to enable such journeys is violet, but a particular pink bordering on violet serves that function for me. Finding out what works for you through experimentation is practical magic.

The Effect of Each Color

The chart (opposite) lists the meanings and associations (affirmations) that I assign to certain colors. It is a personal record. I do not suggest that you follow it but rather that you do your own chart. You must experiment with various colors to see how they affect you. Find out what works most powerfully for you. Of course, there are those who will tell you what each color means, but that is nonsense. Color is a huge spectrum of electromagnetic wavelengths. My blue is not your blue. You are the source of your magic and not some outside expert!

Color as an Element of Practice

Colors are seldom used on their own by magicians. Instead, we choose colors as an element of practice along with dance, song, scents, symbols, numbers, drumming, or chanting. When we move to Part Three, you will draw on this toolbox of practices and integrate them into ceremonies. Practical magicians are creative chefs, always seeking to incorporate a new ingredient into their mix of practices.

SOME MEANING I ASSIGN TO COLORS AND MY AFFIRMATIONS		
Color	Associations I make	Affirmation
WHITE	All round protection, purging evil	Infuse me with white light
YELLOW	Restores emotional health, invigorates, increases happiness, fun	Beam me a smile
GREEN	Attracts abundance, restores harmony, heals and nurtures	Abundance is mine
BLUE	Heightens intuition, protects against evil spirits, brings peace	I am at one with the divine light
VIOLET	Intensifies spiritual experiences, intuition, and healing, brings peace, involved in astral travel	I welcome new experiences
RED	Brings enthusiasm, fun, warmth, intensity, invites play and passion	I want to play (feel it in your tail bone)
PINK	Love, femininity, sexuality (feminine), restores lightness of being	Everything is sexy
ORANGE	Builds immunity to disease, fights off infection, restores sexuality (male)	Color me healthy

★ JOURNEY 14 ★

Do you want to see which colors work best for you or offer the most powerful experience? Review the color chart and breathe each color in and out (as you imagine it) for one-minute, noting their effects. Remember, what you call blue is not universal. Take it slow, observe how each color makes you feel and document each one in your magic journal. Just use your mind's eye to breathe each color. That is how it works because imagined colors can be as powerful as real ones.

Then, of all the colors, choose the one having the greatest impact upon you, for a more intensive session of deep rhythmic breathing (5–10 minutes). Date your journal entry and describe the color, the ritual and its impact. Why did that particular color benefit you? How was it of benefit?

CHAPTER 15

ИPLOY MAGIC NUMBERS

Numbers are so magical that a specialized branch of magicians; numerologists, offer advice on the values, ratios and quantities required for success in sports, writing, music, construction, design, relationships, gambling and other endeavors. The basic numbers are 0–9 and the rest are derivatives. So, it is typical to add the digits of larger numbers into a single digit so that 27 is actually $2 + 7 = 9$. However, 10, 11, 12, and 13 are usually treated differently. For instance, I do not see 12 as 3 but rather see it as a number indicating 'completion' on a higher, more spiritual, order (e.g. the 12 disciples).

How I Use Numbers in Practical Magic

Numbers help me with decision-making. For example, two people make for a perfect romance, but three people are normally better for business partnerships. Four is good for a nice dinner with friends but five can see a division (e.g. someone who feels left out of discussion). A party might include 12 ($1 + 2 = 3$, which is completion) as opposed to 23 ($2 + 3 = 5$) which can breed conflict or polarity. I even choose parking spaces, lockers at the gym, a lotto card or a house (think of the address) according to numerological values.

Numerical Associations

I am not a numerologist (a specialist field) but since my youth, I have done card readings based on numerical values. I learned this technique from a very old woman I met when I got lost in the huge underground marketplace of Teheran in about 1978! She was an empath like me and used her empathic abilities to read ordinary playing cards. I was simply scared, lost and needed help and ran across her and she helped me. She read my cards for a fee. Yet when I asked her to teach me her method, she did. I found that learning the wonders of everyday playing cards enhanced my empathic abilities. I use the card layout to explain and illustrate my empathic findings, although the cards also suggest things to discuss.

In my readings, I lay out the entire pack (13 playing cards per suit, plus two jokers) to help others discover *patterns* in their lives. It is less about the individual cards than the entire layout. I examine the pattern in the layout as the key to people's higher selves. I am reading empathically but also using cards as they fall out to trigger feelings and illustrate what I am feeling. The patterns arise to tell me but are not the primary source of my readings. They augment an empathic gift.

The chart (below) shows the associations I make with certain numbers. Some of these values you will find in standard numerology, as well, but they were taken from a mysterious old lady in a marketplace! Some do not fit. In translation from cards to numerology, the King is 0, Ace is 1, the Jack is 11, the Queen is 12, and the Joker is 13. The rest are taken at the face value given.

#	NUMEROLOGIAL ASSOCIATIONS FOR MY CARD READINGS
0	King: eternal, boundless, limitless, great power for transformation
1	Ace: a new beginning, unity, solidarity, leadership, focus
2	Partnership, romance, renewal, but also duality, polarity, divisions
3	Completion, union, divinity, power to manifest, moving forward with ideas
4	Balance, stability, practicality, four seasons, direction
5	Moving forward, progressive, change, new direction, adventure, risk, mystery
6	Healing, nurturance, overcoming the past, beauty, moving forward
7	High energy, good luck, high spiritual vibration, illumination
8	Infinity, risky, entrepreneurial, cyclic, karmic, a quandary, incomplete
9	Romance, compassion, new ambitions, hope, idealism
10	Creative evolution, the development of an idea, a new start (similar to 1)
11	Jack: good luck, peace, intuition, idealism, honesty
12	Queen: birth, motherhood, a number signifying completion on a higher order than 3 – spiritual achievement
13	The Joker: luck, change, new opportunities arising (fear of change gave 13 a bad reputation)

Other Tips on Using Magic Numbers

Which is more powerful, an odd or even number? Often, I find it is the odd number! If speaking, making one point or three seems to catch more attention than making two. One candle or three candles is usually better than two. Which is more powerful as a visual representation: the symbol 7 or spelling out the word seven? Usually the symbol. So, when adding power to rituals, an odd number tends to have a stronger vibration and employing the numeral (i.e. 9) is more visually effective than the word (i.e. nine).

★ JOURNEY 15 ★

Try using a number (see this chapter) and a color (see previous chapter) to bring success in any small endeavor. Test out your skills but be creative. Select numbers and colors according to the outcome you seek. For instance, if you want to see success on a planned date, then choose 9 (new beginnings) and arrange the time of the date as 9. Wear nine items of red. Include 3 red objects (union, completion) in the event such as a rose, red wine and a red glass. In your journal, explain: your objective, how you employed numbers and the outcome attained.

CHAPTER 16

GATHER YOUR TOTEMS

To be creative, we first have an inspiration (invisible) and then take it to material form (manifestation). A spirit moves through us first, prior to the material manifestation. Does that suggest there is a less visible spiritual world, another realm, behind our shifting material reality? In practical magic, it is possible to relate to the spirit or 'idea' behind each plant, animal, bird, insect, reptile, fish, angel, long extinct entities (dinosaurs), ancestor, departed relative and even beings that might never have manifested (dragons). While many people deny that a spirit realm exists, the very highlight of magic practice for me is making friends in the spirit world!

What is a Totem?

Totems include the entire kingdom of earthly beings: every species of plant, animal, bird, reptile, fish, or insect. They are living beings of the spirit world that include all creatures that have ever existed including those long extinct (dinosaurs) and fanciful (e.g. dragons). The difference is that the totem is the collective living spirit that animates all members of a species. A single dove might bring you a message, but it comes from the collective spirit of all doves.

Choosing a Totem

First, always welcome those animals and beings that naturally come to you as very special. They are primary totems. Otherwise, totems can be chosen, and the usual purpose is to either enhance a desirable quality in a magician's character or to fill a gap in personal power owing to a character weakness. For example, a magician who needs courage might call upon the lion totem.

With practical magic, we must ask ourselves what the totem means to us. You must only adopt totems that you can love daily so that they appear when you call upon them. This is a very personal matter but to assist in explanation, I have bulleted below an idea of how someone might employ particular totems (six examples):

★ The bee totem can bring a spirit of industriousness

★ The elephant totem can remind you of past lessons

★ Ants can help you with the spirit of keeping order and warn you of disorder in your life

★ The eagle totem can help make you be far-sighted

★ The owl totem can bring wisdom

★ The coyote can help you to be clever

The Ideal Number of Totems

The number of totems that you call upon relates to your character. It is common to have about five but since one must stay in touch with a totem, I find five to be too many. Three at a time is quite enough. Perhaps a dog for loyalty; a giraffe for far seeing abilities; and an elephant to steer clear of danger. The easiest path to working with totems might be to select the one or ones that you can remember because those are the ones that stick around. Do not forget pets or animals that are already in your life as these make powerful totems.

Tips for Working with Totems

Respect and love will draw a totem near and add power to your magic but if you do not respect or remember them, they will not stay with you (wear a symbol of them as a reminder). The best and most loyal totems owe to a natural attraction. For instance, I am loyal and easily attract and retain dogs as a totem. The fiercely independent magician might attract cats in the same way. Arrogance, which includes a lack of faith, repels totems. I recommend never talking to others about them, as doing so is likely to invite contempt (owing to ignorance) from the uninitiated and undermine this developing relationship.

Other Potential Friends in the Spirit World

Spirits are not just totems. We can call on ancestors, fairies, spirit animals, angels, guides and a vast number of other beings who dwell in the spirit world (other dimensions). There are techniques such as the trance (we explore that in Section Three), which allows us to enter these realms. Raising one's frequency helps to 'lift the veil'.

★ JOURNEY 16 ★

Are you ready to identify your totems? Identify any three non-human species — such as plant, animal, bird, insect, or fish — that attract you strongly. Do not study the options, brainstorm the choices or rationalize a choice because attraction owing to spirit and heart, is stronger than attraction owing to thought. Test that out by documenting five species that attract you like a magnet.

Second, draw each one in your journal — one per page. If you feel uncomfortable about drawing, paste in photos or drawings, perhaps from magazines.

Third, consult your own heart and spirit (no reading on the subject) to answer three questions per page and per spirit being:

★ What powers are unique to this friend from the spirit world?

★ How does each spirit friend enhance, build, or complement your particular character?

★ How can these spirit friends enhance your magic?

Fourth, thank these friends from the spirit world who came to you when called. Consider designing something to wear that reminds you of your friends in the spirit world.

Finally, conclude your journal entry by stating something about all three spirit friends. Will you be able to maintain all three as friends? How can you be sure that you will remember and honor them? If you cannot, you need to reduce the number of them.

CHAPTER 17

CHARMS, TALISMANS, AMULETS AND SYMBOLS

An ancient magic practice is finding or making an object to wear, carry, or view daily so that it either repels what you do not want or attracts what you do want. Let's review four such objects:

★ **CHARMS:**   these attract good things into your life

★ **AMULETS:**   these provide protection from danger

★ **TALISMANS:**   these are objects that have no intrinsic magic until consecrated (e.g. inscribing words or pictures or making it magical in ceremony)

★ **SYMBOL:**   these have no inherent magical qualities but help us to hold in our consciousness something we want to manifest (a reminder)

How to Use Charms

Charms are usually small objects such as feathers, buttons, sticks, coins, herbs or stones that intrinsically store good luck or beneficial energy. We know it is special and keep it nearby for good luck or to help with manifestation. Carrying a four-leaf clover for good luck is a famous example.

Charms deserve respect for having their own life cycle. For instance, do not fret upon losing one. Realize that the charm is taking a short journey with you and when it leaves, it is time to move on! Avoid expensive charms, if investment concerns you, as high expenditures are unnecessary. You can attract and find very powerful charms that cost you nothing. Since you should surrender them when they accomplish their mission, I would not invest too much money in them.

How to Use Amulets

Amulets generally refer to items that offer protection such as keeping evil people, diseases or misfortune at bay. Many ancient Romans wore amber to protect themselves from evil. The ankh, used by ancient Egyptians to ward off illness, disease and old age, is made of gold and usually inscribed with symbols for long life and protection. Metal and stone are popular especially for inscribing the amulet, but any material is possible.

How to Use Talismans

When magic is not given in the object, you consecrate it in ritual so that it is infused with magic, which is a talisman. For example an object can be consecrated under a waxing moon ceremony that includes bathing, preparing a space and ultimately inscribing the talisman with symbols or writing. We might take a stone, give it energy in a ceremony, inscribe it with the five elements and hang it around our neck. An acorn, consecrated, strung and worn around the neck can be just as powerful and remind the wearer to focus on healing and renewal, either psychologically or physically. Traditional materials might have been animal in origin such as a tiger tooth. Today we might realize, more than in the past, that magic power is less in the object and more in the consciousness of the magician. The talisman trains us to focus our powers.

How to Use Symbols

The symbol reminds us of our intention and therefore helps us manifest it through persistent visualization. For instance, we might stick a dollar bill onto the bathroom mirror to remind us of our mission to attract more income. The bill has no intrinsic value but instead directs us, consciously or unconsciously, to focus more time on income generating opportunities. It is persistence in envisioning that brings your wish to fruition. So, every time we see it, we focus both our conscious and subconscious minds upon the intent.

Some people wear these symbols on their bodies as a necklace or bracelet. Symbols can be pinned to your clothes too or tattooed on your body. The best place for the symbol is wherever it helps you to stay conscious of your intent (e.g. posted on a bedroom wall, bathroom mirror, strung around the neck or wrist). The symbol does not have to be elaborate. Wanting to lose weight, we might draw an 'X' on a piece of paper and post it with a magnet to the refrigerator door. Every time you approach the refrigerator, the symbol reinforces your intention to slow up on eating.

Finding the Symbol that is Right for you

Here is a simple way to find the right symbol: just Google magic symbols! You will get explanations and pictures or diagrams of the symbols. It works because finding the symbols best suited to your character requires original research. Of many thousands of symbols, you need to find the one that registers well with your consciousness. It should serve as an easy and friendly reminder to see your wish manifest. So, move in the direction of taking ownership of the search for the symbol that works best on you. The more you own the magic, the more you develop magical powers (explaining all the journeys in this volume).

Examples of Symbols

Listed in the table (below) are eight common symbols to provide examples of what you might find:

EIGHT SYMBOLS COMMONLY USED IN MAGIC PRACTICE	
Symbol	Association
All-seeing eye	Spiritual insight, higher knowledge, all seeing eye of God
Ankh	Eternal life, rebirth, life
Circle	Healing, renewal, wholeness, unity
Quartered circle	Earth, air, fire and water; the four directions, sacred space
Lightning bolt	Supernatural powers
Pentacle	The five elements, witches, protection against evil
Phoenix (bird)	Rebirth, resurrection, immortality, renewal
Triangle	Number 3; fire; male power (if pointed up)

Choosing the Right Charm, Talisman, Amulet or Symbol

We are naturally (or subconsciously) attracted to the charms, talismans, amulets or symbols that suit us. So, in initially choosing them, do not think too much. The right one will grab you, viscerally, at a deep level. Then, decipher why afterwards. Your very attraction reveals something about your own needs. Of course, you can go another way and declare a strong need or intent and then research the appropriate assistance. Either way, you will learn more about yourself, which makes researching it fun and fun is essential to making magic work for you.

While the best guide to your choice of charm, talisman, amulet or symbol might be natural attraction, you must follow up with research to make very sure that any chosen items match your intent. You might discard certain of these items if research indicates they are associated with negative energies. Such discoveries are not unfortunate but of great benefit because one day, as a matured magician, you might need to identify and remove negative symbols planted in and around dwellings to attract evil entities! So, gladly research objects selected by attraction because it builds your capacity as a magician while offering some protection from poor choices.

When to Let go of a Charm, Talisman, Amulet or Symbol

These objects are very useful for periods of our lives but seldom forever. Perhaps you wear a charm to attract someone, bring luck or deal with some issue. Once achieved, you might lose the object. An Ankh (an Egyptian symbol for eternal life) might remind you that life is eternal, reducing the fear of death, which subconsciously plagues many people. If the Ankh disappears, you might find your fear of death did too. We often lose charms, talisman, amulets and symbols when they are no longer needed. Losing them can say, 'you have arrived at your destination!'

★ JOURNEY 17 ★

Can you find a magical object such as a feather, stone or gem already imbued with some magical quality? You might have something already magical around your house. You might get lucky and find something in your local environment. See what jumps up at you from the beach, the mountain, the ground or the neighborhood. In searching, go with what attracts you immediately, without thought. Do not read about what each item is supposed to do. Rather, find the object that attracts you most powerfully. Focus on its power without deciding what that is.

If you find nothing, that is fine as you can also design and make a symbol out of found materials or consecrate an object as a talisman. Give either a try because it increases your skill set and saves you time and possibly money searching for something already magical. The talisman involves ritual, which is the final section of this book but, for now, a prayer or a few words will do. Blessing your own creation can be most powerful.

Once you locate or make the object, decide where to place it. Popular spots are the ankle, wrist, neck or head. Otherwise, we post such objects to walls, appliances, mirrors or any place routinely visible.

Once you have made your choices, take a photograph or draw the object and paste it into your journal. Describe what attracted you to it, how you found it or how you made it, and the meaning you attach to it. Then, wear it for a day or two, before finalizing the journal entry. Return to explain the experience and value of wearing it.

CHAPTER 18

MAKE USE OF CRYSTALS

Magicians treat crystals as something more magical than a charm, amulet, talisman or symbol because they seem to have life-like energy. It is claimed that crystals have the same hexagonal structure as DNA, draw sustenance from the earth, grow, interact with people and environments, emit positive energy and absorb negative energy. For many centuries, crystals have been reputed to help us heal (e.g. rose quartz might help with cell regeneration), become more mentally agile (e.g. 'rubies make one shrewd') or attract good luck (e.g. fluorite lifts our spirit or promotes spiritual bonds).

How Crystals Work

Crystals form under intense underground pressures over long periods of time to produce a highly ordered mineral structure with a pure and sustained vibration or electric field. The vibration is so regular that silicon crystals are used for our watches, computers and optic fibers. Perhaps the crystal's regular release of energy drives away irregular disturbances of spirit, soul, heart, mind or body.

Types of crystals

Crystals come in more sizes, shapes, colors and prices than can be named but there are about 200 types. Some crystals are semi-precious or precious stones like amethyst, diamond, jade, opal, quartz, tourmaline, emerald, fluorites, and rubies. However, the most common crystal employed in magic is ridiculously affordable: ordinary table salt. A crystalline structure made of sodium and chloride; salt is spread around in a circle to create a protected zone for ceremony. Sometimes it is sprinkled at the door for protection. You have probably soaked your feet in Epsom Salts, crystals made of magnesium and sulfur, that are excellent for healing. Another cheap and common source of crystals: beach sand.

How to Employ Crystals

Our particular needs guide our uses of crystals. Many people place crystals around electronic equipment, such as computers, to deflect emitted radiation. For instance, I live in a drought prone region with water shortages and small packets of quartz crystals are sold here to improve the quality of drinking water. If I see a plant is not doing well, I place quartz crystals in the soil next to the plant. Many people hang crystals around their neck to keep negative people and energy away or to attract something beneficial. Hanging them close to the heart is reputed to amplify the crystal's energy.

Cleansing a Crystal?

My philosophy on crystals is that they are alive and should come and go as they please. I do not hang onto them but instead let them go when the job is done. So, I keep them for a time and am happy to lose them. I do not seek to refresh them but return them to the mountain where I gather them. I do not invest in them monetarily and do not see them as my property. When a crystal disappears or becomes fatigued, I do not rush out to find another one. I do not feel sad. Rather, I accept that the crystal, upon doing its job, departed. To me, gratefully surrendering crystals before embarking on new journeys is vital to understanding how to work with them. The need for another crystal might arise but letting them go when the time is right is also part of the process. You can even let crystals come to you when you need them.

I am not promoting my particular ways with crystals and realize that many people buy precious crystals and want to refresh the ones that have been absorbing negative energy for a long while. They might soak them for a day in sunlight; soak them in moonlight overnight or leave them buried for a day in the earth. Some soak them in seawater while others see that as blasphemy (salt can erode a crystal)! I believe in everyone finding their own way rather than following codes, rules and ideas belonging to others. However, if you spend time with a crystal, you might grow more sensitive to it and realize when it is fatigued. Then, you can refresh it your way. My way is to return it to nature!

An open display of your crystal has a drawback: people, upon seeing it, want to touch it! So, when I wear a crystal, I hang it under my shirt so that people do not see it or touch it.

Can you Offer Examples of Crystals and their Uses?

Below is a chart showing the benefits of ten different crystals. Today's journey will ask you to do some research and design a similar chart but one tailored to your needs. So, reflect upon this chart but less for the particular benefits derived and more for understanding the huge range of crystals and their magical uses. You might want to consider the format too, so that you can construct something similar for your magic journal.

	A SAMPLE OF 10 CRYSTALS: CHARACTERISTICS AND PURPOSES		
#	Crystal	Characteristics	Purposes
1	Agate	Blue, a balancing and grounding energy	Broadens perspective, connects you to a wider world
2	Bloodstone	Red, associated with the root chakra and healing	Grounding, helps regulate blood pressure, eases body aches and pains
3	Citrine	Yellow, connects to solar plexus, linked to gut instinct	Very uplifting, confidence booster
4	Clear quartz	Clear, connects to the mind, clears up brain fog	Brings clarity during confused times, offers stamina
5	Garnet	Rich red, works on the heart chakra	Brings passion
6	Jade	Green, works on awareness, opens your eyes to deeper mysteries	Lifts your spirit, motivates, awakens
7	Lapis Lazuli	Blue, promotes intuition	Opens up every form of communication including extradimensional
8	Onyx	Black, offers protection	Improves your confidence and sense of self-esteem, improves decision making
9	Malachite	Green, promotes wealth	Attunes one to health, prosperity and wisdom
10	Turquoise	Turquoise, throat chakra	Great for improving communication, helps us get over colds and sore throats

How to Learn More

A good way to learn about crystals is to scout them out. You will find them in your environment because we are surrounded by them. Our cars, watches, computers, the ground we walk on, beaches, the mountains around us and daily meals (salt) include them. Look around and find crystals! Then, refer to the huge volume of literature on what various crystals do for your health and magic. You can also take what you find to jewelers or rock collectors. It is quite worthwhile to ask others about the crystals that they use or wear since personal stories can be most informative. Besides, being inquisitive is being magical.

★ JOURNEY 18 ★

Research crystals according to your personal needs. Then create a reference chart in your magic journal of five crystals that hold some value for you (use the one provided in the chapter narrative above as a model, if you wish). Consider also searching the internet (recommended), reviewing books, talking to experts or employing any reference available to you for identifying and charting five crystals that might address your issues. The issues can be anything from finding a partner to better health, more courage, improved communication or protection from harm. Bear in mind you want to identify at least one crystal that you can access and test out. Practical magic works through trial and error. You try things out.

Can you now list five crystals that seem promising to you? Once your chart is complete, obtain one of the listed crystals. Document your find by answering two questions: (a) what crystal did you obtain? And (b) why did you choose this one? Next, wear it over a day or a few. Test the crystal to your satisfaction. Then, complete your dated journal entry by explaining the task assigned to your crystal and the result. Did it help with the task assigned to it? Describe your experience.

CHAPTER 19

MAKE MAGIC BY CANDLELIGHT

Candles represent the element of fire and any wish you make with fire, a living entity, helps you to manifest your vision. We blow out the candles on a birthday cake, sending our wish forward on a flame of light. Candles focus our thoughts or send prayers (e.g. at vigils and offerings). We say to someone who is suffering, "we will keep the fires burning" meaning we will keep them in our thoughts and prayers. Burning a candle adds power to those thoughts and words.

The Practical Value of Candles

First, the communion is with fire rather than a candle. Whether a candle flame or the fiery sun, you are worshipping the same light and intelligence. Worshipping with candles is a *practical* choice: what circumstances best facilitate regular worship? You might be in circumstances where there is more privacy outdoors than indoors. Then, worship the direct fire of the sun. Some seek privacy indoors at home. A candle quietly burning in your room is still the element of fire but is unlikely to raise any alarm bells. Adapting to circumstances is part of practical magic and candles can help us fit magic into our lives.

The Colors of Candles

The candle's color can play a role in how it is utilized. In practical magic, we assign meaning to each color because practitioners do not see colors identically. When I say blue, you might envision a dark hue and I might see a very light one. I might see yellow where you see gold. Although language entices us to create discrete and solid categories, color is a vibrational frequency or wave. The table (below) highlights just a few associations typical to certain colors of candles. It is not instruction but stimulus. Let it spark a self-reflective journey: discover the colors that work for you.

ASSOCIATIONS WITH 10 DIFFERENT COLORS OF CANDLES		
	Color	Typical Associations
1	Green	Material matters, business, recovery, renewal, harmony, growth
2	Blue	Healing, success at home, calms, soothes
3	Purple/Violet	Spiritual energy, spiritual healing, Third Eye, visions
4	Red	Passion, sexuality, fertility, love, fire, power, self-confidence
5	Pink	Peace, the feminine, gentility, tenderness
6	Yellow	Fun, friendships, attraction, joy
7	Brown	Associated with the earth, fertility, bounty
8	Black	Protection, wisdom, imagination, reverse curses
9	Grey	Protection, neutralize evil, induce calm
10	White	Purification, protection, clarity, truth, peace

Four Tips on How Best to Make Use of Candles

Here are four recommendations on making use of candles:

★ Light candles right at the start of an indoor ritual to set the mood to your ceremony (e.g. blue and white candles for a sense of peace and harmony)

★ Keep candles of different colors on hand because each color can then play a role in the design of the ritual. For example, in the United States, the money is green and so many burn a green candle to attract money. However, the lack of a certain color should never stop you proceeding with any ritual since it is the candle flame that holds the power to help you visualize and manifest

★ Fat candles that take too long to burn down seem less powerful than many small, thin candles that burn down completely in the course of the ritual. Timing the ritual to conclude with a complete burn brings a sense of satisfaction that helps with manifestation

★ Since many magicians promote and protect the environment, use candles that are organic and not polluting the environment or yourself with petrochemicals

Candles in Big Ceremonies

I am not a ceremonial magician (group magic) but must briefly mention the importance of candles to group ceremonies. They are seldom excluded but are one prop amongst many (such as incense, salt, swords, music, drums and wands). Ceremonial magicians will burn candles to help focus group consciousness. For instance, candles can shift consciousness toward peace and relaxation. My point: candles are versatile and much of their worth depends on how creatively you use them.

★ JOURNEY 19 ★

Today's journey: manifest some vision by talking to fire, a living entity. Start with the vision. What do you want to manifest? Visualize something that is quickly achievable (24–48 hours) so we can test out your skills with candles.

Next, choose candles in the numbers and colors appropriate to your vision. If you have candles of only one color, do not worry. You can dress any available candles with colored paper, cloth or ribbons. Use your imagination, which is a big part of magic. Make it a fun activity too because in magic, joy brings power to manifestation.

Next, arrange a wonderful altar of candles that speak to your vision or what you seek to manifest. Take the time to create an unforgettable altar. Consider details. For instance, you can mark the sides of each candle with a symbol such as a dollar sign if seeking money. Make the arrangement of the candles work for you.

When the altar is complete, take a photograph and paste it into your magic journal or otherwise draw it in. Describe the altar with reference to your photograph or drawing. Explain any symbolism.

Once the altar of candles is described in your journal, you are ready to test it out. Start by lighting all the candles. Then, quietly develop a connection with fire by concentrating on the candles. Then, open communication. You are speaking to the God of Fire such that feeling that sacred connection, with gratitude, is a big part of successful manifestation. So, start with thanks or some words of appreciation for fire. Honor fire with words that are truthful and humble. When the connection seems ripe, offer up your vision to fire. Accept your blessings. Offer thanks. Then, blow out the candles.

In a dated entry in your magic journal, describe: your wish, the altar and all props or elements utilized for this experience. Include illustrations, diagrams, or photographs because you might refer to this journal entry when you start on the design of rituals (Part Three). Manifestation might take a day or two. So, leave some writing space to describe the outcome when ready.

CHAPTER 20

DANCE TO YOUR INNER BEAT

In practical magic, dance is not a pattern of movements like the Tango. Rather, it is individualized soulful movement in the style, pace and manner that increases *your* joy. It need be neither elaborate nor conventional. Without legs or from a wheelchair or bed, you can develop movements that express who you are. Each magician has a unique relationship to the Cosmos and can celebrate that in highly personalized movement. At least in practical magic, no one else has the same dance as you and that, to me, is what makes magic dance special.

The Benefits of Dance for Magic

While dancing is not required of practical magicians, I recommend it. You can commune with the Cosmos through movement, which heightens your appreciation of the Cosmos and your connection with it. You can use dance to align your unique rhythm with that of the Cosmos so that we see who you are in relationship to the sun, stars, natural world and the Cosmos at large. You can dance to the sea, feel touched by a goddess, or dance to the stars until you feel shivers down your spine.

How to Test the Effectiveness of a Magic Dance

If your dance does not lift you or bring joy, it will have no magic power and must be redesigned. For such reasons, you must never copy someone else's dance but rather dance according to your own sense of joy. Your dance does not have to be a grand performance if you are not a grand performer. A quiet person might express gratitude to the sun in a single gracious movement like folding hands in prayer and then pointing them toward our source of light. That is very subtle, a person dancing in their own way, who experiences tremendous joy in one short movement.

Since no one dances like anyone else in practical magic, you must get in touch with who you are (introspect) and find movements that feel both natural and joyous to you. That requires experimentation with movement, which is great fun and one of the best forms of exercise in the world. Dance awakens your body, mind, and soul simultaneously, which makes it a wonderful path to finding magic on your own.

Where to Dance

There is no right place to dance. Some prefer to dance inside and others outside. Using a private interior, you can arrange and represent each element (e.g. salt = earth; lit candle = fire) and then put on the music and dance a ritual into being (perhaps one minute of thanks per element). You can dance outside to the rhythm of nature too. If you have a busy schedule, try designing your dance within ordinary daily activities (see further below). If you lack an exercise program, dance is a big solution: you can practice magic and exercise at the same time!

The Length of the Dance

The regularity of dance is more important than its duration. Three minutes is plenty to start because you have to get into a rhythm. Of course, you are welcome to dance longer but the joy of dancing can also be lost if overdoing it from the start. You want to get a core routine going and then build upon it over time.

Here is an approach you might try: first create a very short dance signature (like a 'tableau' of your dance). Think of it like one to two seconds of your longer dance or a freeze-frame of that dance. The signature is powerful when utilized regularly in social settings as everyone comes to know of that little gesture or movement as you. Perhaps you snap the thumbs and middle fingers of both hands over your head. That is all it takes.

If you start by developing the tableau, you have a foundation for designing the longer dance. You can also develop many tableaus and eventually you have a dance. In other words, you can test out different signature movements to see what works for you and then compile these into the longer dance. A dance signature can also suffice as the dance, especially for those who feel physically challenged to do more. I am not a big dancer and use tableaus.

What if I am Busy and Have No Time to Dance?

You can mix dance into the things you do daily, whether work or play. I pause a moment here and there, amidst other activities, to dance in a manner that usually goes unnoticed by others (tableaus). For instance, I might dance while walking to the shops to buy groceries. I use small, slow and fragmented movements like hands held to the sky, just to amplify my connection to the Cosmos and express gratitude. This little dance with the Cosmos is so short and sweet that it would not register with an outside observer but brings order, calm and clarity to my day. So, I stop, when the right moment arises, just to feel the constant and vibrant exchange of energy between myself and a living universe in a brief set of movements (tableaus). That *is* magic dance!

The Speed of the Dance

Since your dance is not a performance but individual expression in movement, you can go at whatever speed suits you. However, just for educational purposes, realize that a long, highly energetic dance can raise your frequency high enough to enter other realms! Energetic dancing over a time can speed up your frequency to the extent that you can discover elemental beings of earth, atmosphere, fire, water and spirit. I use other techniques but know that a dance can get you into a trance state. Throughout history, many peoples and cultures around the world danced under the stars all night long just for that purpose. However, take it slow to start.

The Health Benefits of Dance

Dance provides a means of exercise, worship and can release all negative energy owing to the free expression of the soul. Those of us who absorb negative energy from people around them, like empaths, can dance that vibe away. I find a convenient spot, preferably outside with abundant fresh air and sunlight. Before anything else, I sometimes stand for a moment to simply soak up sunlight for purification. Then, I slowly turn to face each of the five directions (including up and down). Then, spin. Of course, you can do that at any pace that suits you, but I spin slowly at my age. Try it! You can literally spin out any anxiety while:

★ Thanking, with uplifted arms, the magnificent sunrays as a great creator (fire)

★ Breathing deeply to fill your lungs with the nutrient-rich atmosphere

★ Making joyous movements with your feet, expressing love for the earth that supports you

★ Waving your hand though the air to feel and thank the atmosphere

★ Looking upward into the vastness of space, the source material for all form

Dancing to Fire

When we go outside to dance to the sun, moon, stars or a fire, we are partaking in one of the oldest and most powerful ways, ever, to practice magic. Such outdoor dance ceremonies are legendary in the history of magic and are considered by many to be the best way to communicate with higher energy forms.

A fire dance is a basic part of many magical practices for good reason: it builds inner joy. In many ways, dance is the product of being joyful; the will to dance is an achievement owing to joy. Magic functions best on joy, making dance a big deal. Furthermore, if you lack the will to dance, dance to a fire anyway as it will clear out the dark energy stopping you from dancing! Fire can reshape our energy fields by casting out negative energies. It literally brings light to dark situations. It removes toxic energy, so that you can attract good energy, good people, passion, love, connection, healing and wisdom.

Of course, you do not have to dance around a fire at all. It is a practitioner's choice. Sometimes our choices owe to circumstances rather than solely to our predilections. For instance, outside fires are restricted in many environments, making fire dances near impossible. In designing rituals, make them fit with who you are *and* make best use of your available environments. Those two factors help to define practical magic, which is an expression of the magic within you!

Dance for Manifestation

When magicians want to manifest something very specific, they might use dance. For instance, spinning slowly in different directions like north, east, south and west is a dance acknowledging magic forces including earth, air, fire, water and space. Once we feel a connection, we might then stop to share a concern or desire with the universe. We then conclude with some words of thanks and patiently wait for the right moment for delivery, demonstrating faith.

★ JOURNEY 20 ★

This is a four-part journey to design, execute and document a dance expressing gratitude to the five elements. To start, head up five pages in your journal with the name of each element. Then, under each page heading, describe three important ways each named element enables and facilitates your life.

Now, take your chart and dance into being a way to thank each of the five elements. Don't design the dance but express yourself through movements that represent your gratefulness. For instance, if you are grateful for oxygen, then breathe deep, and thank the atmosphere for it. Let your body move as it naturally wants to but capture these movements in your grimoire so you can later refine the dance. We do not always plot dance moves out on paper beforehand, but it is practical to do so for longer ceremonies. However, this dance should only take five minutes maximum. Do not overdo it.

Upon completing your dance, make a journal entry that illustrates (sketch, photograph, diagram, film) the main movements of your longer dance. Add descriptions to ensure you have captured it accurately.

On a separate page of your grimoire, illustrate your 'signature' movement, which is a pose or a frozen section of your dance or one movement. It can be a short movement of one to two seconds. Hold the position and have a friend photograph it or just sketch it into your journal.

Since this tableau becomes your signature (who you are), I recommend some clear illustrations for future reference. Tableaus are very powerful magic. You can use them in many settings as a form of self-expression declaring your spiritual presence.

CHAPTER 21

GENERATE SOUND AND VIBRATION

Sounds, whether produced by musical instrument (e.g. drumming, strumming) or voice (e.g. singing, chanting), creates a vibration that affects mood, perception and feeling. Vibration is so powerful that opera singers reach pitches that smash glass. Whole cities can be leveled by weapons that issue sound.[1] Of course, a kind magician generates vibes that bring harmony, love and peace. We seek to lift consciousness but never lower it. Let's discuss the magical value of sound and vibration in terms of: (A) music; (B) speech; and (C) the chant.

(A) MUSIC

If music has ever moved you to tears, you will understand that a vibrational frequency or 'vibe' can quickly alter how one feels or thinks. In fact, there is scientific evidence that drumming improves mood and cognitive function; increases the opportunity for mystical experiences; reduces high blood pressure and slows brain degeneration.[2]

How to Find the Music that is Right for you

The sounds that build one's sense of harmony, peace, calm, joy or healing vary per person. In fact, you might know that from playing a musical instrument or just dancing to your favorite sounds. I love spontaneity and on-the-spot magic. To me, music is magic when it is of the moment

---

1   Hamblin, James (23 Aug 2017) 'What are Sound Weapons?' *Atlantic* https://www. theatlantic.com/health/archive/2017/08/sonic-attacks/537714/

2   Sayer, Ji (April 2015) Six Evidence-Based Ways Drumming Heals Body, Mind and Soul. https://wakeup-world.com/2015/04/07/6-evidence-based-ways-drumming-heals-body-mind-and-soul/

or expressed spontaneously. So, when the moment strikes, I hum, sing, whistle or just make sounds from available materials. Today, you will invent music within seconds by tapping on water glasses, filled to various levels to produce amazing sounds. It is quick but works to bring an uplifted mindset that you can carry with you throughout the day. Such an approach fine-tunes your magical skills, lifts your vibration, and helps you recall that inner magician. Making your own sounds from available materials can save you time, money, and avert an unnecessary trip to the shops!

(B) SPEECH

Magic speech refers to the use of the spoken word in magic to:

★   Lift or shift the consciousness of a person or group

★   Reinvigorate mind and body

★   Induce happiness

★   Promote positive thinking

Words have power and are known, scientifically, to assist with healing and positive transformation. For example, just telling ourselves 'to heal' can promote real healing.[3] I think we have all seen that a funny word or a humorous reference can transform a tense moment into shared laugher.

The Names we Give Ourselves

The names that we give ourselves are magic speech and you can rename yourself to match the frequency that you want to emit. It works like a mantra, yielding tremendous power, because it is repeated back to you whenever anyone calls out to you. You grow richer in that chosen frequency as people call out your new name! Of course, not all magicians should rename themselves. I use my birth name, Rich, which is short for Richard. I reassigned meaning to my name to attract what I need as I need it. I accepted myself as 'rich'.

---

3   Wade, Theresa (27 Apr 2017) 'Heal Yourself by Talking to Your Body' https://uplift-connect.com/heal-yourself-by-talking-to-your-body/

Magic Speech in the Design of Ceremonies or Rituals

Discussing magic speech helps to bridge the gap to the next section on ritual because sound and vibration are most common components. Bear three things in mind:

★ Few words, used sparingly, often have more impact than many

★ Magic speech is seldom used alone but enters into a mix of practices

★ Since you are the one lifting the energy, the way you make the sound (the vibration you emit) is more important than the actual word selected

This use of speech, combined with other ritualistic components, such as dancing energetically about the room full of joy, can transform a negative space into a light-happy one. Magic speech can lift *you* into such a positive frame of mind that you bubble over with light, channeling it everywhere to overwhelm all negativity.

If negativity lingers in a room after the departure of very negative people or events, then a purification ritual is required. You might light candles around the room and spin into a dance wherein you spray wonderful scents while speaking out-loud to all five directions. You might say to the sun 'fire this room with light' as you throw open the curtains or use mirrors to bring in light. While opening windows or turning on fans, you might say to the atmosphere, 'purify this place'. To the earth, while spreading salt on the floor, you might say, 'protect me with your presence'. To space, you say, while joyfully dancing, 'restore spirit here'. You might shout out, 'wash away the past' while cleansing the space with water and herbs. So, ritualistic cleansing of a negative place involves a combination of techniques in which magic speech can play a part.

Tips for the Effective Use of Magic Speech in Ritual

Here are four tips:

★ Choose only a few words or phrases to include in your rituals rather than whole sentences

★ Do not choose words for their dictionary definition but rather for their emotive content, intensity, resonance or the ability to create an intended vibration. Some magicians even use archaic languages and meaningless words such as waving a wand and saying 'abracadabra' ('I create what I speak') knowing full well that few participants speak ancient Hebrew

★ During the ceremony, stress the intonations that have the most emotional resonance for what you want to achieve. For instance, if driving an evil spirit out of a house, you do not want kindness in your tone but rather throw salt and repeat in a firm tone 'be gone!' but without losing your sense of inner joy

★ To lift a targeted group or a friend to a happier state using magic speech, it helps to know a little bit about that group or friend. Interview them or inspect their home or work life

Magic Speech for Liberation

In the magic that I practice, which I call nature magic, joy is the essential source of magic power. Joy comes from finding the connection between your unique soul and the Cosmos. It helps to drive out unproductive ideas (spells) implanted in our heads through socialization or upbringing. For example, we might have listened to repeated words, definitions, or concepts describing success in popular culture that do not really match our inner feelings. Rather, we unwittingly picked up this contrary chant or mantra through socialization. We say to ourselves silently "I need to fit myself into the job market." If that mantra does not suit you, repeating it can cause lifelong anxiety and undermine the free expression of your character. Perhaps you belong on a farm or as part of an intentional community. So, it is of great value to self-observe and review any unproductive chants that stifle the real you. Once you see one, immediately countermand it with a better chant that will liberate you. Perhaps say from heart to self: "I will live in freedom, thank you!"

(C) THE CHANT

Chants, the repetition of sounds at a certain vibrational frequency, do much work in magic. Yet it is not the words that matter most. Rather, words, often rhyming ones, given in a certain pitch can call forth nature spirits, create a better atmosphere, improve your mood, develop magic powers, excite, calm, heal, manifest something or help you to find wisdom. We can chant mantras, affirmations or statements that make us think more positively or that energize our bodies so that we can see more of the hidden and high-vibe world around us.[4]

We hear much today about people using plant medicines, like Ayahuasca, to explore other realms and meet up with deities, supernatural beings or 'friends' but the most reliable and ancient method for such journeys is the chant. This is not to diminish the value of plant medicines but to say that the chant assists, as powerfully, to enter into alternative states without the need to purchase, find or consume plants that are not always available or safe. You do not need to depend on them. You have the chant, a system so powerful that it can lift you onto higher planes, take you into other realms, and help you to astral travel.

Who Uses a Chant?

Chants are used by all kinds of magicians, shaman, traditional peoples, sorcerers, witches, covens, Buddhist monks, Hare Krishna, Hindus and meditation experts. Those well practiced in the trance can shift their vibration sufficient to seeing into or entering adjacent dimensions. On the other hand, beginners struggle to chant correctly, usually focusing too much on word meaning and too little on vibratory quality.

---

4   Lively, Katherine (2014) 'Affirmations: The Why, What, How and What If' https:// www.psychologytoday.com/us/blog/smart-relationships/201403/affirmations-the-why-what-how-and-what-if

Making a Chant Effective

As a self-trained nature magician, I feel chanting alone works better and easier than chanting in a group. However, many collectives have chanted together to achieve the vibrational frequency for entering the trance. So, there are many paths to learning the chant. Here are four tips on how to make the chant work for you at home:

★ Think of a chant as communicating with the spirit realm through vibration. It is not about the words but the vibration they emit through repetition. For instance, the most popular chant of all, the sound known as 'om', seems to invite the sacred

★ Do not include many different chants because the repetition of a given vibration delivered via a single chant has more power. It is so powerful that sticking to the same vibration can attract beings inhabiting other realms

★ A chant is normally just one of many elements contributing to a ritual. So, combine other elements like a color. 'Violet-violet heals the body, violet-violet heals the body' is a chant I use to direct my own healing (violet works for me). I envision the color *and* a healed, happy me while chanting

★ Be true to yourself. A good chant requires authenticity while those who speak in an affected manner lack magic power. For this reason, in the distant past, children often led group chants owing to the authenticity of their voices. Use your authentic voice. How? For me, it means finding my inner joy and expressing that in my voice. Joy is key to explaining the power behind all nature magic. If there is no joy in ritual, the nature magician should stop and redesign it, rather than continue

Practice Makes Perfect

Magicians coordinate and integrate various magic practices and tools to bring power to their rituals and ceremonies. For example, chanting while drumming can be more powerful than the chant alone. However, chanting first requires practice on its own to get it right. If you chant to free yourself of negative energy or employ the chant to clear a room of negative vibes, you are developing skills important to magic ritual.

★ JOURNEY 21 ★

To discover sounds and vibrations that work magically for you, test out three methods today (magical sounds, magic speech and the chant).

First, conjure some magical sounds utilizing items found in and around your own home such as wine glasses, pans, forks, jars and anything else easily available to you, including your voice and hands. A quick exercise is needed to demonstrate the power of this. I recommend you grab some wine glasses (thin glass is best) and a spoon or metal utensil and make music within seconds by tapping on glasses, filled with water of various levels to produce amazing sounds. Whatever you choose, grab something convenient or familiar to you to make sound (a saw, chopsticks, a drum). Harmonize them to create a musical piece of no more than 1–2 minutes. In your journal: document the materials that you utilized; the sound you created, especially in terms of shifting your feelings, perceptions, mood, and consciousness; and the impact your sounds had on you or the world around you (e.g. targeted people or places).

Secondly, redirect yourself, someone else or a group to a more joyful place using the power of magic speech. Select any quick situation to target, perhaps at home, work or elsewhere. You can target yourself or others. If you do include others, you do not have to inform them. Rather, make sure all techniques fit with the targeted people or situation such as changing a negative consciousness into a light-filled one. Stress magic speech but feel free to use other components such as happy music, uplifting photos, humor, flowers or artwork. Finally, in your journal, describe: the magic speech you used, its appropriateness to the targeted people or situation, and the impact. To improve future practice, note what worked and what did not. Include sketches, photographs, or diagrams to illustrate the outcome.

Thirdly, design a chant and test out your skills at chanting. First, set an intention for your chant. Then invent a short chant that meets your intention. Describe it in your grimoire and establish a location for it. The *best* location depends on what you seek. If you want to 'enchant' your garden so that it grows magically, that will take place outside. Begin your dated journal entry right now with: (a) a statement of intent; (b) an illustration of the outcome that you envision; (c) the chant; and (d) why that chant is appropriate to what you want to manifest. In design, you can include other practices that you have liked so far, such as dance or healing crystals.

Upon completing the design, execute the chant. Continue until you feel you have accomplished your mission but do not go overly long (5 minutes maximum) on this first test of yours. Upon completing the chanting ceremony, finalize Part C of your journal entry. Make sure that you have described:

★ Your intention and target (e.g. reviving the dying plant)

★ The chant (write it out)

★ Location (consider a photograph)

★ Any other components of the chant (list)

★ The outcome or result (did the execution match the plan? What happened?)

★ Ways you might improve upon the chant

If necessary, leave additional space in your magic journal to comment on any outcome still awaited.

★ PART THREE ★

DESIGN MAGIC RITUALS

CHAPTER 22

CRAFTING A RITUAL

Today's chapter is a launching board into ritual. Crafting rituals that match your naturally magical ways takes time and experience. So, to get you started, I employ the chapter narrative to describe and explain some steps typical of any ritual. Then, for the journey, I will guide you through a short, more specific ritual thanking the five elements for the gift of life. This process has you entering a very basic ritual into your magic journal that you can tweak in the coming chapters to suit your naturally magical ways.

Understanding Intent

In practical magic, your intent (owing to character, outlook, beliefs and more) can have a big impact on the design and outcome of your rituals. Some employ rituals to get what they want, like love, money, success, a car or a sense of peace. Some use rituals to harm their enemies, which goes against the first principle in magic; 'first, do no harm'. Rather than harm anyone or ask for anything material, I use ritual to create a sense of harmony between myself and the grand intelligence of the Cosmos. To me, ritual is the art of communion with the divine. My aim with it is to expand consciousness and reunify with the source. Similarly, you must know your intentions (reflect upon this) as it will have a major impact on how you design rituals.

Some Basic Steps in a Generic Ritual

Practical magicians are not bound to any rules, except do no harm. Still, there seem to be some typical steps in the design of rituals. Let's discuss these steps (below) that also form the chapter subheadings (in bold caps further below) so that you can envision or understand a basic ritual and then creatively expand upon it. Note that I am sharing my own ways, which includes much elemental magic (worship of the elements), but after understanding a basic ritual (the chapter narrative) and designing one for practice (the journey), you can accept or reject anything you see here:

1. Purify the space
2. Purify mind and body
3. Open the circle
4. Commune with the elements
5. Thank the elements
6. Close the circle
7. Reground and purify

STEP ONE: PURFY THE SPACE

Many of us purify both place (step one) and person (step two, further below) for three main reasons: (a) to avoid attracting unwanted beings; (b) to avoid negative energy; and (c) to prevent dark moods. Some spread salt in a circle for 'protection' from negative energy or entities and conduct the ceremony inside that circle. To purify one's body, you might bathe in herbs, dance and don fresh clothes. Let's start with purifying the space, since that is where many start the process, and then discuss purifying mind and body.

It is typical for new magicians to want to skip purification and just get on with the ritual. I often did. I employed the basement of my house for rituals because it offered privacy while spirits, fairies and elementals showed up very well under the reduced light. I doubted that I would attract negative entities as I had never had such an experience. My 'friends' were just there to help me! Well, one day I got chased, harassed and victimized with nowhere to run and no support because no one around me (then) would have ever understood such a predicament. I felt attacked by demons and it was agonizing.

Through my failings, I realized that there are some fairies, elementals, spirits, demons and other entities too mean for us to want to summon. They can be very scary and in the worst scenario, can scratch you or fool you into harming yourself. I love fairies but visiting them is somewhat complex as they come in colonies, some of which are not so nice. Then, there are demons that deliberately and gladly harm you. There are also some wandering spirits that you need to leave alone. After death and for various reasons, certain humans prefer to be light, bodiless, souls that linger as 'ghosts' in places that involved some past matter they did not quite understand. I would not disturb them!

In terms of demanding purification, there are three types of settings in ascending importance: (a) outdoors; (b) indoors with some lighting; and (c) a very dark space with low lighting.

Purification Outdoors

The need for purification outdoors depends on your location, season, timing or quality of sunlight. Some outdoor spots offer purification rather than require it. I know of a protective circle of boulders, right on the beach (full of natural crystals) that absorb and radiate sunlight (a purifier). These rocks are constantly sprayed by the sea (water, salt crystals) while fresh oxygen (air) whips all around. That powerful concoction of elements, all in one spot under strong daylight sun, creates a purifying situation where dark energies cannot easily take hold.

Not all outdoor rituals are held in the daytime but are under the moon or stars at night. One wants nothing underfoot when in the dark and so we tend to clear away any debris to create a clean and open space under the night sky. Big outdoor fires are not always possible but can expel the cold, replace negative energy with positive energy and create a natural circle of safety. One can use indoor techniques like spreading salts, herbs, crystals or some mixture of them in a protective circle, but in my view, lighting a big bonfire cannot be bettered for clearing out negative energy at night. It seems to offer natural purification and protection over a long period. In fact, such fires, from time immemorial, have attracted humans seeking safety.

Purifying an Indoor Space

The first step for indoor rituals, where potential dangers are higher than outdoors, is purification and protection. To purify the space, you need to cleanse it well. Remember that dirt and grime are attractive to negative entities. So, clean the environment of any past residue, stale air, dirty floors or leftover angst.

Be clear about the exact spot where you will conduct the ceremony as that saves time. Clearly demarcate a space. Then, clean, clean, clean.

Invest time in making it sacred. The floor must be thoroughly cleansed but not with toxic chemicals. Rather, use natural herb mixtures like sage, lavender and rosemary, or salt-water, apple cider vinegar or lemon. I sometimes grab needles off a giant rosemary bush nearby, spreading them all around. I find the store-bought items to be less powerful than what I find freely available in nature or just at home. Other cleansing formulas and ways can be found on the internet or in books.

Addressing the atmosphere or air is also important. Many people smudge the environment with sage, which cleans the air amazingly well. Smudging sticks are very easy to order online too. Other ideas include chiming, joyful music of any kind, sprinkling salt or crystals, moving sunlight into the room (mirrors can be used), airing the room, vigorous dance and spraying consecrated water. What works for one person does not necessarily work for the next. A practical magician might conduct research (e.g. books, online research, communication with colleagues) and experiment to find the ways that work best for their own character, their natural magic. Furthermore, recording *both* your successes and failures in a magic journal is equally useful. Never complain about a failure because it is great information! In fact, practical magic really proceeds by trial and error. So, do not avoid failure but bless it and dutifully record it.

Once dirt and grime have been removed, demarcate a circle using salt or some mixture. You can use stones, herbs, crystals or candles too. Light candles all around because natural light should replace all artificial light. I tend to use a bed for elevation and comfort. I am senior and need to forget about my body to commune properly. So, I spread a combination of herbs, salts and candles around and conduct the ceremony on a bed from inside a protected circle. Each of us is unique. Many practitioners face an altar of some kind. You can do that. The best technique is the one that feels right to you.

Preparing an Indoor Space to Avoid Negative Entities

There are times when rituals *require* much darkness. For instance, a dark environment assists us in seeing beings of light from other realms. The downside: many negative entities also like darkness. So, purification becomes more intense, sometimes requiring days of planning.

Here are five ways to keep negative entities at bay in an indoor setting:

★ Smudge the entire place to drive out negative energy It is powerful and very easy to buy smudge sticks. One can make smudge sticks from herbs (e.g. dried sage or lavender) too. One advantage of smudging is that it purifies you as well as the room

★ Use an aromatic dispenser to spread essential oils throughout the space such as rosemary basil, eucalyptus, lemongrass or lavender. These offer protection and lift your mood, which is important as joy is a magic force of great power

★ Use mirrors to shine strong sunlight from the outside into the dark spaces inside. Flooding the space with sunlight makes me feel secure and I might do it for hours. My intuition tells me when the negative energy has lifted

★ Employ sound as a great cleanser. You can chant, sing, chime bells, drum or play any musical instrument to break up and clear out negative energy in a space. You replace negative energy with positivity through joyous sound. You can dance to these sounds as well, which amps up the impact. How joyous you feel is a wonderful barometer of success in cleansing the space

★ A protective circle for the ceremony is a very widespread practice. Some insist on it, but this is practical magic and you can do as you like. Some use salt, crystals, stones, dried herbs or lit candles to shape the circle

STEP TWO: PURIFY MIND AND BODY

Perhaps it is harder to free your mind of negative thinking, anxieties and stress than to relax the body but either one can undermine the ritual (e.g. attract negative entities). However, relaxing the body, relaxes the mind and vice-versa. So, I will discuss them together.

You cannot follow someone else's instructions as to how to ground yourself and bring calm to mind and body. It will naturally differ between people. I can tell you what I might do. If indoors, I do a first-stage purification ceremony, cleansing body and mind about 24 hours beforehand, and a late-stage one (a bath or shower) just prior to ritual. The earlier purification involves whatever technique (e.g. dancing, singing, mediating, deep breathing of fresh air, bathing in water, etc.), learnt through trial and error, that offers the best cleansing experience. I tried many techniques but dancing on rocks near the sea did the most to clear out negative energy. Perhaps the salt crystals that abound in that environment create the right vibration for purification. A swim in the sea might do the same or any moving water body, such as a river or a cascading waterfall, works. Another time-honored way is relaxing in the sun. You know that you are purifying body and mind when your spirit lifts. So, you must experiment to discover your own ways, the practices that work best for you.

The last thing many do before embarking on the ritual is bathe. Perhaps enjoy a warm bath full of flowers and scents surrounded by white candles. I shower, since I am in a drought-prone environment. Water, in most forms, helps much for purification and is the basis of my preparations. Praise this living goddess for her work by treating her graciously during the ceremony. Gratitude is a superpower in magic. Offer thanks.

STEP THREE: OPEN THE CIRCLE

Many practitioners open ceremonies from a magic circle subdivided into five directions (east, south, west, north, and up and down). They send thoughts and words in the direction of each deity to thank them for their gifts. In ceremony, we are speaking to deities. A tip: write out your words of thanks in advance or at least know what you are thankful for and take the time to design beautiful ceremonies accordingly. Grace and gratitude are the right state of mind for practicing magic properly. Life disappears in the absence of even one of these deities (e.g. without spirit, we evaporate instantly). Know that and you will be gracious and offer proper thanks upon opening the circle.

STEP FOUR: COMMUNE WITH THE ELEMENTS

When we approach the elements of life, I see gods and goddesses and would never affront them with a laundry list of wants and needs. Rather, I stay present with them and let my relationship evolve as one does with a friend. If you take your journey (below) that way, communion starts out best with gratitude. Those who are gracious might prioritize gratitude or offering thanks for the gifts bestowed upon them by these deities of earth, air, fire, water and space.

Let your relationship with the elements evolve through communion. Let your magic evolve. Magic becomes more beautiful, effortlessly, with daily communion. A unique relationship evolves between you and the elements that becomes a major source of magic power. So, my advice is to prioritize communion, keep it going, and let your practice evolve with love and imagination. Trust communion. To me, it is not the means to an end, but it is where magic begins and ends.

STEP FIVE: THANK THE ELEMENTS

Upon completing your visit, thank the elements one at a time in reverse direction. Start with space (up and down) and then move north (earth), west (water), south (fire) and back to east (air), where you started. Thank them with heart and spirit and let them go.

STEP SIX: CLOSE THE CIRCLE

Break the circle and release any residual energy from the ceremony back to the world. Know that your mission was accomplished and have faith. Let it go.

STEP SEVEN: REGROUND AND PURIFY

Following ritual, many of us find a way to return to the secular world. Depending upon your circumstances, you might first need to remove materials and return the space to normal. If I hold a ceremony in an indoor setting, I often wander outside into the elements to 'reground'. Some might just breathe deeply. Others might bathe again. Some take a nap or rest awhile in the sun.

★ JOURNEY 22 ★

The chapter (above) described one style of ritual that might or might not suit you. It is reference material or information to build upon and you should use this chapter to guide you for the remainder of this workbook.

Below, I provide more reference material by expediting you through the steps of designing a more specific ritual of gratitude to earth, atmosphere, fire, water, and space for the gift of life. Just follow my directions so that you capture a basic ritual in your magic journal, providing a template for all that follows in the workbook. You will modify this basic ritual, draw from other sources, including your own soul, until it suits your naturally magical ways, but you need something to build upon. So, document this well.

First, study the rooms or spaces available to you at least 24 hours before the ritual. Select a good indoor location with complete privacy and no chance of interruption. If you live alone or have lots of privacy, this is not a problem. Otherwise, you must scout out a space.

Second, cleanse the space thoroughly, floor and atmosphere, as detailed in the narrative above. You have to make up a cleaning mixture. Herbal potions or mixtures with an added natural scent, like lavender or rosemary oil, are good. Make up a mixture that brings you joy. Start out with the floors. As you clean them, attune yourself to the vibe of the space. Is the space becoming more harmonious or not? If not, choose other techniques as discussed in today's narrative (above).

Third, demarcate a circle where you will conduct the ceremony using any of the materials described in the narrative such as salt, herbs or a combination. The circle should elicit a sense of beauty, peace, safety and comfort. You should not want for anything once the ritual starts. So, have sufficient space and gather all materials for planned activities. Many create an altar to give them a strong focus. It is popular but not required. Some, like me, never use an altar. Your preferences will become clear to you over time as you try various approaches.

Fourth, take a photograph of the prepared space upon completion. Just paste a photo, drawing or illustration of some kind into your magic journal for a record of the purified space so that you can later reflect upon the ceremony and improve its design. Be precise, neat and include every detail in your entry since it is the template for future purification ceremonies (a feature of all chapters ahead). List every tool, prop, herb, mirror, and material required for the initial ceremony so that you can later build upon it.

Now, design into your magic journal a five-minute ritual expressing gratitude to earth, atmosphere, fire, water, and space for the gift of life. You might want to write some poetic words extolling these gods and goddesses. What do you appreciate about each? List whatever tools, herbs or equipment you need. Once you have drafted the ritual into your journal, gather any additional materials and put them in place. Then stop.

Just prior to ritual, go take a bath, a shower, swim, bathe in the sun or otherwise get ready for ceremony. Anoint yourself with herbal salts, herbal preparations or scents. Calm the mind too and wear fresh clothes. Document everything with photographs and list all materials utilized.

Next, conduct a five-minute ritual of gratitude for the five elements (see the chapter content for details). Start your ceremony from inside the circle, asking the five elements to bless your space. Remember you are speaking to gods and goddesses (be humble, worship these beings that give us life). Also, call out to any allies in the spirit realm — spirit guides, ancestors, totems and any spirits already close to you — to protect you on your journey into magic ritual. Listen and be with them silently but only for a few minutes. Document any messages received.

That is enough action for today. Thank the elements. Close the circle. Reground and purify.

Into your journal, document and detail every aspect of the ritual including:

★ Photographs or drawings of every item employed

★ Words, music, chants, colors or materials effectively used

★ Anything that was not effective

★ Anything that was missing

★ Any improvements to be made next time

Magicians record every detail in their magic journals so they can later review and refine practice. That is why you need to be self-critical: did your purification ceremony work? Did it help clear your being of negativity or not? Did it build your inner light? If it felt awkward in parts, that is to be expected. Eloquence does not usually describe one's first ritual. Rather, we evolve with practice. Since our practices improve over time, your first ritual *will* be cruder than subsequent ones. So, always note in your magic journal what improvements are needed for rituals of this kind.

CHAPTER 23

UPLIFT CONSCIOUSNESS

Any day of the week, you might see people walk, run, meditate, dance, or sunbathe to feel happier, restore a sense of harmony, or heal. Magicians engage in similar activities to uplift their consciousness, but their approach is more disciplined and includes more design elements. A bit like a scientist, a magician tests out rituals, documents all methods, props and tools in a journal, evaluates success or failure with each, and then concludes the entry with ways to improve practice. On today's journey, you will design, test out and document a consciousness-raising ritual that you can refine and improve upon for years to come.

Maintaining a High Consciousness

Everyone has up-and-down days, but a magician can employ ritual to keep that consciousness a little higher, a little longer. How do you define a high consciousness? To me, it is based on joy: the more joy, the more uplifted the consciousness. So, I design rituals to produce joy until my consciousness is so uplifted that I can see it lifting those around me too.

Rather than borrow another person's method for maintaining a high consciousness, I recommend finding out what maximizes *your* joy. Perhaps it is a morning meditation, a dunk in the ocean, or a walk on the hillside during a sunlit morning. Perhaps it is expressing gratitude from a quiet bed before parting with your blanket in the morning. There is no right way to find joy. You must experiment with what feeds your soul, using joy as your barometer. Whatever makes you more joyful is lifting your consciousness and expanding your magic powers.

Ritual for a Higher Consciousness

A basic consciousness-raising method in magic is communing with nature. We can regularize and perfect that communion with ritual. That means that we design the interaction, observe its impact, and document what works, improving practice. To me, ritual is a just a disciplined approach to working with nature.

The regularity of the ritual is more important than the length of it. So, rather than designing long rituals to start, emphasize short, fun, and easy ones that fit seamlessly into your daily schedule. A short ritual of five minutes every morning might be easy for you and is sufficient to keeping you uplifted throughout the day. You might light a candle beside your bed and say a brief prayer every morning or night or head outside daily on a work break just to worship the beautiful sky, land or ocean. Start out simple like that. One day it leads to an all-night ceremony under the moon and stars! What is important is integrating ritual into daily life and that takes time. So, I am advising you not to overdo it in the beginning. To integrate ritual into your daily life, make it easy and fun.

Joy: The Magic Barometer

The essential mindset for making magic effective is joy. Practical magic works better with joy as the driver as opposed to discipline or pressure. For instance, if you love your rituals, take photos of them, write about them, illustrate them and otherwise engage joyfully with your magic journal, you will not have to be disciplined. Instead, your love of ritual will drive you. No technique is very powerful if it is not practiced daily but making it fun raises your consciousness so sky high that you will not have to force yourself to do anything. The sheer joy of practice will drive you rather than discipline per se.

To me, joy really comes from being at one with nature, spirit, or the divine intelligence. Our consciousness naturally expands and uplifts through connection to the source, creating joy. The source of all energy on our planet, the origin of nature as we know it, is the sun. So, at least once a day, as part of a disciplined practice to build joy and heighten magical abilities, I worship the sun, which feels like a reunification or a coming home. Only a few seconds or minutes a day is required as it lifts your consciousness fast. The regularity of it is much more important than long rituals on rare occasions. If this appeals to you, integrate sun worship in a way that is easy for you so that you do it routinely.

Raising the Consciousness of a Group

It is not always necessary to address the consciousness of others if you are building your own light. When you are full of light and joy from ritual, you will automatically lift group consciousness by your very presence. One can blast away at negativity without even knowing it. Magic ritual uplifts consciousness, which can have a positive impact on any group. Being full of light from ritual can help a collective without necessarily targeting them or ever mentioning the word magic or ritual to them. If you worship nature every day to lift your energy, it gets re-expressed as humor, laughter, gestures, storytelling, dance, beauty, harmony or just open-hearted ways. By building the light in yourself, you help uplift others automatically.

Can a magician uplift group consciousness? Yes. Collective issues can be resolved when individuals agree to cooperate in lifting group consciousness. In my career as a criminologist (a social scientist working to prevent crime problems), I used a bit of magic. I found that many community-based crime problems were resolved by helping community members lift their consciousness so they could partner and cooperate. I would audit the available people, skills, resources and budgets already available to resolve crime issues and present them to communities. This raised the collective consciousness, led to teambuilding, and resulted in highly successful community safety plans. Rather than offer solutions, I lifted the consciousness of community members so that they could resolve their own issues. So, you can, indeed, lift both your own consciousness and that of a targeted group.

★ JOURNEY 23 ★

Let's use ritual to uplift your consciousness and then test it out in a group setting to see if your uplifted consciousness has an impact on others.

First, identify and analyze any negativity that you hold in your consciousness about money, work, self, co-workers, friends or family members. Is there any inner tension that you would like to see resolved once and for all? Define the challenge so clearly that the existence of it or the usefulness of addressing it is beyond debate. Enter your findings into your journal.

Secondly, design a short five-minute ritual to dispel negative energy and increase your joy. The objective is to produce joy through color, smell, dance, stones, chant, or any other method that works for you. Review your magic journal and identify the techniques that worked best for you. Then design a 'ritual for upliftment' into your journal and list all components, step-by-step, starting with purification and protection.

Third, carry out the 'ritual for upliftment'. Then give thanks, close the circle and reground. After re-grounding, did you feel more joyous? You should feel much more joyous as that was the objective of ceremony. You can redo a ritual if you did not obtain the desired result.

Fourth, as a test of efficacy, share your uplifted energy with others. Find another person or two to be with to demonstrate to yourself whether or not the ritual made you more joyous. The impact of heightened consciousness owing to ritual is that we express more joy. Perhaps we share a fun story, skit, poem, song, joke, tale or flowers. Raise the light within your own being, monitor that joy within you, and see if it does not help uplift those around you. Usually, it will.

Finally, describe the conscious raising ritual in your journal. What negativity did you address? Did you turn darkness into light? Review your entry and make sure you have listed and explained every step that you took including preparation, purification and protection, giving thanks to the elements and five directions, delivery and closure. Did you use any props? Explain how well the ritual worked in terms of each component. Did uplifting your energy have any noticeable impact on others? What did not work? Note in your magic journal anything that you would change so that you keep improving your rituals.

CHAPTER 24

DESIGN A HEALING RITUAL

Designing a healing ritual well depends upon correctly identifying one's elemental imbalances. This chapter will be a short pep talk because you already know how to do this but might not realize it. In a seven-chapter effort to define your elemental mix in Section One (Chapter 2–8), you learned how to identify your elemental weaknesses and rebalance your energies by invoking the missing element. Once you identify the missing element(s), you can design beautiful healing rituals that invoke the missing element into your being.

Review your magic journal. Look at what you have learned about color, number, dance, speech, candles, herbs, the five elements, the five directions, charms, crystals and more. Do you think you can combine some of these practices to create a healing ritual aimed at balancing the elements within you? You might have to self-diagnose. If wet or cold, you might design a ritual of fire to 'invoke' dry and warm. If your lungs were congested, you might invoke fresh air. If your bloodstream needs purifying, you might drink herbal teas (water, earth) to flush out the toxins and heal. Perhaps you are mentally agitated and take a rosewater bath to bring a sense of harmony. If despondent, you can invoke high spirits through a joyful ritual of fire and dance.

Joyful Ritual

Healing can be achieved through joyful ritual, which helps to create positivity, the environment in which healing occurs. By creating joy, you empower yourself to heal, balance and regenerate mind, body, spirit, heart and soul. Joy maximizes the power of ritual. Ways to generate it have already been discussed in previous chapters.

Examine and Address the Setting

We are not always the source of our own illness. The societies or environments in which we live can produce disease (e.g. think of air pollution). So, we consider the physical, social, cultural and economic setting and look at how to create a balance of the five elements in our place or situation. We might bring in light if it is too dark, remove toxic substances from the environment or get the air circulating.

Taking responsibility for healing

These days, owing to advertising and the massive influence of pharmaceutical companies, it is easy to surrender too much power to profit-driven medicine but in doing so, you lose track of your natural capacity to heal. Of course, we should listen to experts, but we should also recognize that we are also the experts on ourselves. No one knows you better than you. We observe ourselves more holistically than others might, often understanding certain details, unknown to others, that promote healing. Furthermore, the person afflicted with the disease has the strongest desire to get rid of it. Strong intent is crucial to success in magic and a big reason we should take ultimate responsibility for our own afflictions.

Magic and Healing Others

By reclaiming and joyfully expressing your inner magician, you are on the path to becoming more of a healing presence. Magic raises your vibration and sometimes the mere presence of a high vibe person is sufficient to lift, heal and inspire another. By healing yourself with magic you influence others to do the same. In that manner, self-healing helps to heal the world.

★ JOURNEY 24 ★

Identify any imbalance in your being, whether physical, emotional, thought-based, passion-based or imaginative. What specific element is most weak? Are you lacking in earth, air, fire, water or spirit? Today, I would like you to invoke any element that has been weak in your being and become stronger. Through worship, you rebalance your energies. Perhaps if you need more fire, you can design and hold a ritual outdoors under the sun or by a fire.

This process starts with reflection. Take cognizance of your entire person (spiritually, emotionally, physically, mentally and soulfully) to ask, what element can restore harmony to your character today? Where are you out of sorts? Is it your thinking (air), enthusiasm (spirit), body (earth), passions (fire) or emotions (water)?

Now, into your journal, design a ceremony that helps you to grow stronger in the element where you are weak. For instance, if too spacey and not earthy enough, design an earth ritual to ground yourself. The ritual does not have to be something extraordinary. You can ground yourself in such easy ways as spreading salt in a circle around you, orienting yourself to the five directions, or by worshipping the particular element in which you are weak. Start with purification and follow all the steps in designing rituals. Open with an expression of gratitude to each of the five elements but design the ritual to invoke that weaker element more strongly into your being.

Be creative with sound, color, dance, chant, numbers and other components but keep the ritual short for learning purposes. Concentrate your time on design. Write everything out in advance and be creative. For example, you might bring an object representing the 'weak' element into ritual, consecrate it during ritual and wear it afterwards.

Carry out the healing ceremony from inside the circle. At closure, remember to take the circle down.

In your journal, explain the purpose of the healing ritual. What element were you trying to invoke and why? Make sure you captured each step in the ritual starting with purification and protection. Review all elements of design including any props that you used. Identify and list any changes required so you know how to make the ritual even better next time. Add illustrations, photos or diagrams so that you have an easy way to improve your ritual at a later date. Be neat.

CHAPTER 25

CONJURATION

There are several connotations to the word conjuration. First, humans can 'conjure' or manifest anything, material or non-material, including humor, healing, joy, a vision, an event, money or a new car.

Secondly, one can also invoke (take in) the healing light of the universe in outdoor ritual and then re-channel it (evocation) to the world to:

★   Bring joy where there was fear

★   Furnish knowledge where there was ignorance

★   Build health where there had been disease

★   Restore harmony where there was disharmony

★   Channel light where darkness prevails

Thirdly, conjuration can also mean taking aboard a certain quality of life energy. For instance, I can call upon a spirit animal, like the owl, to bring wisdom. I conjure the real spirit of the owl (the collective) and inject it into my being. I become more like the owl and a bit wiser owing to that *invocation*. We will invoke a spirit animal for today's journey since it is a very safe thing to do and an easy way to demonstrate the power of conjuration.

A fourth sense of the term conjuration is contacting extradimensional beings. We are in a huge universe with trillions of expressions of life. Most are unknown to us. We can 'conjure' the presence of a tiny portion of them but that is enough to be the highlight of anyone's practice! It has been the highlight of mine. In particular, I spend a lot of time with fairy folk although there are many other non-human life forms that can be conjured. It is doubtful that your 'journeys' will be the same as mine but upon maturing into magic, you will, at some point, encounter intelligent beings from adjacent dimensions. Magic can take you there.

Basic Rules of Conjuration

Let me review some practices (bulleted below) essential to effective conjuration:

★ Safety Practices for Conjuration

★ Setting the Intent

★ Visualizing the Outcome

★ The Conjuration Ritual

★ Responding to the Opportunity Moment

STEP ONE: SAFETY PRACTICES FOR CONJURATION

Some forms of conjuration are not only super safe but offer protection from harm such as invoking the right elemental balance of earth, air, fire, water and spirit. Millions of people all over the world tell of safely evoking ancestors or spirit guides to help them in a time of conflict. Invoking totems, such as the spirit of the lion to find courage, is very safe. Many magicians invoke light, a cosmic intelligence, to drive away negative feelings, beings and energy while also healing and heightening awareness. That is not only safe but offers massive amounts of protection.

It is always risky to conjure individual spirits, departed loved ones, fairies and certain elementals. I once had a massage therapist with whom I used to do trades. During a therapy session, we discussed her experience with visiting entities. I listened and understood she was not being fanciful. So, I explained to her how to use purification and protection, which she thought was silly. These visiting spirits loved her, and I was not understanding that! I later heard that this very bright girl suffered a fright so severe that those close to her admitted her to a mental facility. She did recover but, like many who suffer such scares, she never tried conjuration again.

Infestation by dark energies usually owes to a practitioner who is: (a) having a bad day with too much negativity; (b) employing magic for selfish gains such as wealth, power, or pleasures only for themselves;

and (c) not employing purification and protection. Regarding the first point, never hold a ritual if you are feeling negative. On the second point, when we obsess on material desires, we are worshipping a false god (e.g. money), which is the lure by which phony kinds of magic operate. In my practice, I am neither greedy nor selfish but work on what is good for all. 'First, do not harm' is the prime directive in the 'nature magic' (my term) that I practice, which means that I only conjure or manifest that which brings us into harmony with nature. On the third point, never skip purification and protection.

Let me outline five safety practices particularly important to conjuration:

First, take no shortcuts on purification and protection. The worst thing that happens is probably infestation by negative energies. They can surround you and not leave you alone, influencing your thoughts and behavior. To avoid such encounters, prepare for your ceremonies properly, as explained in this workbook. Then, your chances of ever encountering them are low.

The second safety practice is to be full of light from daily ritual. Then, you are less likely to encounter dark spirits. We can invoke strong light, mainly from the sun in daytime rituals, and then evoke that light energy, which can see negative entities flee. The light shining from the eyes of those who engage in routine ritual hurts them! If you are strong of light, your chances of encountering them are very low.

Third, poor character produces poor magic. So, magicians give up ego, greed, selfishness, arrogance, lust, pride and other deadly sins to discover a cosmic consciousness, a superior intelligence to which we can surrender. Rather than directing nature, we become one with it through ritual. So, in conjuration we are not acting selfishly but in concert with a divine intelligence. We align with nature and invoke its intelligence, which is a very powerful practice for bringing safety.

Fourth, as light-filled people, magicians are powerful warriors who, without thinking much, automatically change the alchemy of places and people from negative to positive. They also have an arsenal of techniques and practices (e.g. light, fire, mirrors, dance, sheer goodness, etc.) and, if in serious trouble, they can conjure help in the form of angels, elementals, beings of light and other high spiritual beings.

Lastly, you can ask another magician to help you if ever overwhelmed. I once called upon an indigenous magician in South Africa (known as a 'Sangoma'), now deceased, who helped me to drive out some entities surrounding me. I was being lazy and not spending sufficient time on purification and protection. My friend, who communicated with entities, told me they had been sent by a detractor. We worked together to flood them with light, herbs, sound and dance. He chanted in African languages while smoking the entities with herbal mixtures for about two hours until they departed. So, when in serious trouble, turn to another magician who can double your capacity to remove negative entities. It worked for me quite a few years ago, which was the last time I was troubled.

STEP TWO: SETTING THE INTENT

The living universe is the force behind conjuration. Setting clear intent and communicating it well to the Cosmos, delivers. Unfortunately, poorly considered intentions are more common than clear ones. So, we need to consider intent very well (see further below). You also support your intentions with belief. If you believe your prayers will be answered, that is the result. You have to intend success or align yourself with the vibration of success (belief) to realize a positive outcome.

Perhaps the hardest part about intent is knowing what you want. We think we know but, usually, do not. We say we want to be wealthy when our real desire is no stress in meeting our needs, which might come from a loving community rather than a bank account. We say we want sex when we really want love. We say we want a sports car when we really want a convenient system of transport. Owing to advertising, social conditioning and other forces, your stated desire might not be what you really want, which can add up to years of wasted rituals. This is why the first third of the workbook was on deprogramming. To know our real intentions and practice magic successfully, we must listen to the call of our own souls and cannot do that when our brains are filled with centuries of indoctrination.

To be clear about your intent, ask what do my heart and soul say as opposed to my socialized brain? Who is the real me? Upon serious reflection (take your time), you might find that you have always had a sense of purpose that drives you, a deep life intent, a deep desire, that has followed you from birth. Go deeply into that because that is your magic. Our characters are unique, with individual purpose, and setting our intent to match that character is all powerful. Sometimes we can remember that purpose by reflecting upon our early life history before we got derailed by propaganda and false belief systems.

In my case, I reflected deep to see that my wants, desires and fears owe to social conditioning, something to be expunged if you want to free your soul to practice magic. The conjuration I practice is not for me but for everyone, all life, the whole Cosmos. That owes to a shift in consciousness from 'me' to 'I am the Cosmos', which brings powerful universal forces into alignment. By communing with nature, an all-knowing and higher intelligence, I discovered myself as part of the grand design of the universe. I have a role to play! As I start acting in harmony with that plan, I discover healing, joy and the ability to conjure.

STEP THREE: VISUALIZING THE OUTCOME

Once you have clear intent, the second step that enables conjuration is visualization. A vision is a mental image, an imagining, which we can put into symbols, pictures, drawings, models or plans. For example, if transport to work in a distant location is needed, post a picture (e.g., a photo or drawing) on a wall or mirror of you arriving at your destination successfully. This technique allows the universe to work out the details for you. Then, you will see that unforeseen opportunities arise (e.g., the employer offers to fly you there, lifts are arranged with co-workers, or you receive money for public transport). If you restrict yourself to one idea (I need a Jaguar) or instruct the universe, it can restrict your opportunities and slows down manifestation.

STEP FOUR: THE CONJURATION RITUAL OUTCOME

In many ways, conjuration is 'letting go' so that your will is manifested. We must let our intentions go to the universe and have faith. The period of delivery, being unknown, can test our faith. We must not harass divine intelligence or nature but wait for it to deliver what is best not just to ourselves but to all concerned with the matter at hand. In that wait, many become impatient and abandon their dreams, which causes the conjuration to fail. By losing faith, we lose the power to conjure.

All over the world, people conjure angels, ancestors, departed loved ones and spirit beings. However, the Western world, owing to its history of 'rational' discourse, might have more doubters than we see in the East (China, India, etc.). To build your faith, see that consciousness is the portal to the world that we see and create around us. All kinds of spiritual people, from metaphysicians to shaman, use the power of consciousness to conjure living energies of various kinds including the five elements. Keep the faith, keep practicing, and you can experience these wonders too.

STEP FIVE: RESPONDING TO THE OPPORTUNITY MOMENT

After the ritual, I release the vision and then patiently await the exact moment for taking gracious receipt of what has been visualized. That moment must be acknowledged, acted upon and the creative intelligence of the universe thanked. If you do not respond to the opportunity moment, you lose what you were seeking.

★ ★ ★

Conjuring Extradimensional Beings

Conjuration to attract extradimensional beings includes two types: (A) *evocation* or summoning spirits that bring positive energy; and (B) *invocation* or the act of bringing into oneself a certain life spirit to assist with a matter. Regular practice with both forms of conjuration can expand awareness, heal disease, resolve crises, bring wisdom, restore nature, create harmony, reverse spells and bring light to places gone dark. Invocation also assists with manifesting dreams. I believe these forms of conjuration have been practiced for the greatest part of human history.

Conjuration is not as simple as snapping one's fingers. You must know what you are doing to succeed. It took me years of practice to contact extradimensional beings. Since human beings are very heavy in material terms, I have my doubts that anyone travels to other dimensions. Personally, I have been visited by extradimensional beings. They enter my spaces such that I have doubts about the human capacity to travel to their worlds. I could be wrong, but that is my honest experience.

Remember, too, that one's powers to conjure are limited by one's beliefs. If you believe you cannot conjure, that is the outcome. These are also required: discipline (mind and body); frequency (you must raise your energy levels); humility (a trait essential to attracting friends from adjacent dimensions) and experimentation (repeated practice).

Recognizing a Presence

A presence from another dimension is seldom visually sharp at first. One learns through practice how to see ethereal beings. They do not stand before you as humans because they are not human. I suspect that empaths or psychics have an advantage in making this connection. Why? The first 'sight' of beings from other dimensions usually arrives in your heart, guts or bones. It can take some time to fully identify what you are seeing physically because other dimensions or beings at other energy levels are not functioning like earth-bound humans. It is with practice that those dimensions become clearer and clearer. Then, one day, like riding a bicycle, you quit thinking about technique and just automatically see, even completely forgetting the process that got you there.

Time, Discipline and Practice

I regard conjuration as a very sophisticated achievement, which requires time, discipline, and practice. Routine worship, perhaps daily, turns the magician into a light-bearer, who can help invoke and evoke the universal harmony of fire, air, earth, water and space. Light, a product of fire, is particularly important to me as it is via light that I developed an awareness of living beings that most people do not see. Not all intelligent beings are carbon based like humans. Some are beings of fire. For decades, I have regularly interacted with such beings from nearby dimensions, but especially fairies (a certain group of them). Contacting them is the highlight of my practice. Your practice will not be like mine, but you can experiment to see what works for you. With time, discipline and practice, you can learn to enter the spirit world, which is vast and beyond measure. What you find is *unlikely* to be what I find.

☆ JOURNEY 25 ☆

Let's practice conjuration in the safest way possible, which is to invoke a spirit animal. This also offers tremendous value, a companion for life. However, you must remember your spirit friend daily. They are real spiritual beings but go away if you lose focus on them.

First, at the top of a blank page in your journal, enter a characteristic that you would like to amplify in your character such as kindness or bravery. Next, choose the appropriate totem. For instance, to invite loyalty into your relationships, call on the dog totem. If you want to improve your memory, call on the elephant totem. If you are seeking bravery, perhaps the totem should be a lion. Explain clearly in your journal what characteristic you are trying to invoke and why. I recommend that you adopt up to three totems in this lesson (repeat this exercise three times to obtain three totems).

Next, in your journal, design an invocation ritual to bring this quality deeper into your being by employing all learning to date. Remember that all rituals start with purification, protection and gratitude.

Finally, carry out your ritual. The objective is to invoke each spirit animal into yourself using the ritual that you designed. Feel the outcome from within your character (e.g. did invoking the spirit of the lion make you feel brave?). Date your entry and describe both the ritual and each outcome (per spirit animal) accurately in your journal. Later chapters will offer opportunities to reflect upon this journey and improve upon your invocation technique.

CHAPTER 26

CONJURE WITH FIRE

The source of fire on earth is the sun, a deity so powerful that each one of us, including the sensory impaired, can feel this energy from 93 million miles away.[5] We do not smell or hear over such distances but daily we are caressed by a distant star that creates our greatest earthly treasures such as light, the seasons, ocean currents, weather, water, air, plants, food, animals and people.

The sun also infuses matter with life. For instance, the sun interacts with earth, the mother of humankind, to produce a particle-charged atmosphere of life-yielding elements, such as oxygen, which you breathe about 17,000–24,000 times a day just to stay alive.[6]

Of course, our sun is but one small star in a vast and fiery universe. The bigger deity is the cosmic fire (it is all connected), which is usually part of any magic ritual along with earth/matter, water/fluid, air/atmosphere and spirit/space. Fire is responsible for light. While estimated to be less than 5% of the universe, a small quantity of light is very powerful compared to the darkness.[7] For example, the sun churns up, compresses and expands space (the darkness) to create motion, forms and shapes.

Fire as a Creative Intelligence

When we commune with light, we are communing with photons of fire, the same entity that shaped the earth and brought us life. Amongst the trillions of stars, our sun is small and yet it powers our entire solar system. Without its fire and light, everything would be lifeless, which tells us of

5   Sharp, Tim (19 Oct 2017) 'How Far is the Earth from the Sun?' https://www.space.com/17081-how-far-is-earth-from-the-sun.html

6   Reference (24 Mar 2020) 'How Many Breaths Does and Average Human Breathe Per Day?' https://www.reference.com/science/many-times-average-human-breath-day-d3a07adf198e4794Re

7   McCrae, Mike (October 2017) 'Astronomers Have Finally Found Most of the Universe's Missing Matter" https://www.sciencealert.com/astronomers-finally-found-90-percent-of-the-universe-s-visible-matter

the unfathomable power of fire in this universe. We can learn more about this power and the extent of it through worship. To nearly all magicians, fire, including the sun, is a creative intelligence worthy of worship.

I discovered fire by relating to elementals of fire, real beings who are living expressions of fire or fire-dominant beings. They contain all five elements rather than being composed exclusively of light, but they move around in iridescent bubbles, shiny orbs that they can compress together or expand apart to create shapes, almost anything imaginable. They are intelligent shapeshifters, who taught me much about magic. Many of the illustrations of fairies in books and articles that I have seen show them to be as solid as humans but that is not my experience. They are shapeshifters and illusionists, which might be difficult to fathom at first. Some take the images they create as a hardened reality because humans see hard realities. However, fairies, or the entities that I meet, bend light and constantly assemble and reassemble into new shapes.

If your mindset is to think of fire as a dead, neutral force blindly obeying the laws of physics, you will be deprived of the opportunity to increase your magic powers through worship. Your own thinking will prevent you from speaking to fire as an intelligent deity presenting itself in many forms. It might help you to know that very recent science tells us that sun worshippers see an increase in size of their pineal glands.[8] This produces evidence for a phenomenon long reported by magicians: sun worship assists in intuition. To help such powers grow, many magicians worship a sun-filled morning and express gratitude for the sunset every evening.

Some Basic Characteristics of Fire

While, fire might seem very familiar to you, bear in mind that it manifests as the sun and stars and is coextensive with a universe about which we still know very little. It is a long journey to know fire. Perhaps it distinguishes itself by requiring something to consume. It also purifies, transforms and heals by destroying pathogens. These are some other characteristics of fire:

★ Generates light

★ The energy behind motion

---

8   Shift (2020) 'The Ultimate Guide to the Pineal Gland' https://www.shift.is/pine-al-gland/

★ Stokes the imagination

★ Gives power to words

★ Purifies and destroys

★ Regenerates and renews

★ Provides insight when things seem dark

★ Consumes water (dries)

Representing Fire in Ritual

Since, without fire, there would be no magic and no life, it plays a most powerful role in ritual. Space, earth, water or air change shape under the influence of fire (e.g. water to steam). The atmosphere in a room shifts with just one lit candle.

Quite often, we encircle ourselves with fire (candles sometimes help form the ceremonial circle). Many people use an altar, where they focus much attention during ritual, and seldom is it without a candle. Outdoors, the strong light and warmth of a bonfire might be the central focus for an all-night ceremony. Whether from the flame of a candle, bonfire, cauldron or lantern; fire is so central to magic ritual that it is often the first item to greet the eye.

Conjuration with Fire

The rituals that you design with fire should aim to increase your personal joy but only you know how to find that joy. Through self-observation and worship, learn about the characteristics of fire that attract you and design your ceremony of fire accordingly. What about fire gives *you* joy? Note that and express it in ritual making sure your joy is genuine or you will not draw much power from fire or any other element. The elements are as alive as you and it pays magical dividends to treat them as alive. Joy owes to true communion; that you truly see and appreciate the elements as alive. Then, they appreciate you.

Location

While a fire ritual can be done inside or outside with equivalent outcomes, preparation for the one outside might be more involved. For an inside ritual, we can light candles or burn materials in a caldron but outside we tend to have larger fires requiring items like a shovel, a fire pit, buckets of water (a safety precaution) and a fire permit. One advantage of the outdoor ritual might be the ease with which we can create smoke by tossing materials onto the flame. The smoke adds another component to ceremony like sending our thoughts up in smoke. The advantage to the indoor fire might be privacy and more control over the flame. Outside, during the day, one can use the sun as the source of fire, which I like as it involves no mess to clean up afterwards!

★ JOURNEY 26 ★

This journey has two parts: design and ritual. First, design a ritual to invoke fire into your being. Some might do this to strengthen their characters or to resolve an issue. However, on this journey, let fire take you on a vision quest. The outcome of a fire ritual can easily be a vision because fire speaks that way. I seldom posit questions or seek immediate answers but instead commune with fire for a while, until a vision returns. That way, I listen and commune with a divine intelligence rather than placing orders for things that I want.

Enter the design into your journal with text and drawings. My suggestions are:

★ Always make sure the ritual is appropriate to fire (e.g. a vision quest)

★ Start with purification

★ Use some form of protection like a circle (fire can form the protective circle or be within the circle such as on an altar)

★ Design a way to express gratitude to all the elements (write these down in advance so that you articulate them well, especially the gifts of fire)

★ Include movement, such as dance, since fire loves dance and energy

★ Plan elements appropriate to fire including scents, candles or sage

★ Choose a suitable location and time (will you do it outside at dawn? Sunset? Night? In the light of the day?)

★ Always begin ritual with gratitude (thanks) and conclude the same way (reverse and close the circle)

A tip: newcomers to magic often overemphasize material desires (a capitalist mindset — 'I want a car'), which undermines the power of ritual. Those who see magic as consumerism make assumptions or have expectations that diminish their ability to see, interact, learn and commune. Rather than place demands upon fire, open yourself up to a vision quest. Invoke the 'spirit' of fire into your being first before asking for anything. Then, work with this living intelligence. Let fire stir up your passions and give you a vision that you can take away. Focus upon a flame, a fire, stars or the sun and let your passions go. Sometimes we dance around a fire until the vision presents itself.

Upon completing your fire ritual, describe it in detail including design, execution, all materials used and success or failure. Did a vision return? What did you see? Note in your journal anything you might want to change in future rituals of this kind.

CHAPTER 27

CONJURE WITH EARTH

The term earth does not refer to our planet only but has a universal context: there are earth-like materials throughout the Cosmos. Thus, 'earth' describes the denser mineral matter that comprises all planets, moons, asteroids and heavenly bodies. In that enlarged sense of the word, the real extent of 'earth' and its exact form and nature are not precisely known. However, we can become more familiar by worshipping earth as we know her.

Earth as a Creative Intelligence

Many magicians, being concerned with restoring love and respect for the earth, refer to her as our Mother; a creative and intelligent being that gave birth to humans and trillions of other life forms. Her fertility, stability, healing and provisioning of food, water, heat, minerals and much more, sustains life on this planet. Can we show more reverence for Mother Earth? The fate of humankind might hinge upon that because many people see the earth not as a mother but as a treasure chest of items to grab for quick profit. Such irreverence leads directly to the exploitative behavior that is rapidly destroying a goddess. If enough of us worship her as a creative intelligence, just like magicians do, we might escape the self-destructive path we have taken.

Some Basic Characteristics of Mother Earth

The earth provides for our physical needs. We call upon Mother Earth for healing or when seeking prosperity and abundance. Of the elements, it is the one that brings us back to reality when mentally clouded. Altogether, we appeal to earth when we need to:

★ Ground our thinking

★ Find nourishment

★ Acquire something material

★ Succeed in business

★ Connect to nature

★ Become fertile (e.g. pregnancy)

★ Put out fires

★ Heal the body (medicine)

★ Purify places (e.g. using salts or crystals to create a circle)

Representing Mother Earth in Ritual

In magic, we normally represent Mother Earth in a most natural and easy way. We might sprinkle salt on the ground in a circle or just reach down, pick up some earth and blow her in five directions. Flowers, crystals, acorns, seeds, herbs, stones, a bowl of sand or a rattle are just some of a thousand ways to represent earth in our rituals. You can find items from other traditions too. Although I favor items direct from nature, coins, certain colors of candles (green, brown) and other symbols can represent earth in ritual too.

Conjuration with Mother Earth

Since every individual is a unique expression of life, your relationship to Mother Earth is unique. Take cognizance of your individuality, your gifts from Mother Earth, to conjure successfully. She is proud of you as a unique expression of the natural world and wants you to recognize that in yourself. Once you do, you make a strong earthy connection, which facilitates earth magic. As the son or daughter of Mother Nature, you have natural attractions and tendencies. It might be an attraction to herbs, animals, physical labor, gems, plants or sports. Follow those very natural tendencies and you can find regular success in conjuring with Mother Earth.

Location

You can worship earth from any location or situation. If you can conduct rituals outside during the day using the natural earth, I recommend it because the earthy elements are at maximum power in a natural setting. Outside in the light of day, you can worry less about negative energy and entities. Of course, every location has certain advantages. An indoor earth ritual can be performed quite easily after purification. Since this is about earth, use minerals, salt, gems, stones or soil to create the circle.

★ JOURNEY 27 ★

With great inner joy, design and execute a ritual to commune with the Earth Goddess about something of concern to you. Draw upon your imagination and your journal to design a ritual befitting you and your particular relationship to Mother Earth. Here are some key considerations:

★ List and Illustrate all components of the ritual in your journal first

★ Include purification

★ For protection, demarcate a circle

★ Start the ritual by giving thanks to all the elements but especially for the gifts of the earth (list what you are thankful for in advance)

★ Make sure you are requesting something earthy

★ Commune with the earth on the request (do not insist on certain solutions)

★ Wait for an answer (be patient, listen, observe, watch for signs)

★ Close with thanks and gratitude (reverse the circle)

While you can ask for something specific, be sparing with both words and thoughts. Nature magicians usually commune with the earth about their concerns and then feel the earth or listen. Put your ear to the ground and hear the voice of the earth. Listen also to your own body because you too are part of Mother Earth. Watch for signs overhead and all around. The earth speaks to us through nature, her progeny. Many beings from insects to birds to animals to flowers can carry messages. Take your time as one would in meditation and be very observant.

Give thanks upon concluding the ritual. Did you receive an answer, an idea or an inspiration? Document your ritual thoroughly, include illustrations and explain the results.

CHAPTER 28

CONJURE WITH WATER

Water is about fluidity, malleability, spontaneity, adaptability or natural flow. Once on a journey with water, we adapt to *her* fluid ways. If we are too rigid, we drown in her currents and undercurrents. Better that we set our sails with her and adapt to the changes and flows. Someone might have told you, if you fall into a river, don't fight the current but flow with it. 'Going with the flow' is the way to conjure with water. We trust where it takes us.

Water as a Creative Intelligence

Water is connected to emotional intelligence, heart and feeling. If you get in touch with your heart, you are in touch with the intelligence of water. When we feel the deepest of human feelings (the heart), we see tears (water) flowing out of our eyes. This is because the heart is connected to water and can invoke the power of water to 'wash away' negative feelings. In a holy baptism of water, the Water Goddess cleanses body, mind and soul of sadness, guilt, sins, past errors and painful memories. You conjure a new life by washing away the old one with water. It is a way to get 'unstuck' from people, things and circumstances but *only* if you 'flow along' with the process. Resistance kills the flow.

Some Basic Characteristics of Water

Water is transformative (alchemical). Sometimes it is so transformative that the original intent for which you sought out this goddess, shifts in the process of consulting her. Water helps us shift and adapt. After a negative encounter, many of us shower to wash away the bad vibes. Jumping into a river or the ocean is even more effective. Let me bullet some general characteristics of water:

★ Associated with the heart, emotion, compassion, and love

★ A source of inspiration (think of waterfalls)

★ Detoxifies mind and body

★ A way to dissipate anxiety (a swim, a bath, a cup of tea, a splash of water)

★ Helps us adapt

★ Helps up to expand consciousness (facilitates introspection)

★ Puts out fire (balances the elements)

★ Purifies (preparing for conjuration starts with cleansing ourselves and our spaces with water)

★ Heals and a medium for healing (e.g. infused with herbs)

★ Promotes empathy

★ Associated with intuition and psychic powers (the empath)

Conjuration with Water

We appeal to water when we need to conjure a new beginning. Perhaps you want to release the past, escape the clutches of a manipulator, or leave some negative circumstance, idea, or viewpoint behind. As ritual, you can bathe, swim in the sea or sit under a waterfall but water is so powerful that just a cup of tea (hot water and leaves) can literally 'flush away' the past and evoke a new beginning. That single cup of tea, if treated with sacredness and grace, can transmute an anxious moment into a peaceful one. Stare into the cup, which is a sacred symbol of water, to visualize and manifest a new beginning. Then, with grace and gratefulness, drink the tea you just blessed! After a ritual in a teacup, you can go forth with faith knowing the Water Goddess has your back.

Representing Water in Ritual

Any liquid can represent water. In fact, some use rocks, like aquamarine. Plants that are full of water such as aloe, lemon, water hyacinth or lettuce work well. One way to represent water in ritual is with a cup, chalice or goblet. Some fill the chalice with wine, which they drink during ceremony! Yet, I prefer pure water to any symbol or representation of it. Nature magicians, like myself, tend to go natural but there are many options in the magic community. Magic is as much an art as a discipline. Tip: follow your natural instincts and tendencies so that you gravitate toward what works best for that unique constellation of characteristics that is you.

Location

Location depends on what suits you. Being water-dominant and preferring outdoor and daytime ceremonies, I am always looking out for natural water formations such as rock pools, lakes, rivers or oceans where I can immerse myself (briefly) at some point. However, I undertake many indoor rituals too. It gives me the opportunity to use a very ancient water ritual that I enjoy. I fill a bowl with water and add ingredients that move me that day such as rose petals, salt, crystals, scents, colors or leaves. I then stare long into the bowl seeking messages.

Rather than being carbon copies of one another, magicians tend to develop practices, even a style, that suits them. For instance, many nature magicians, being very independent, adaptable and organic, will make ad hoc use of materials at the particular moment of ritual. We might reach down, spontaneously, and grab sand and throw it in all five directions. Some like less spontaneity and more regularity, which has great value too. Indoor ceremonies can be most convenient for that purpose since one can set up permanent altars, have a selection of ceremonial materials nearby, and take up ritual at regular times.

★ JOURNEY 28 ★

Can you design and execute a joyous ritual focusing on water? You will need an intent such as 'washing away' a negative feeling or emotion that undermines your magic.

Here are some key considerations for the design of your ritual in worship of water:

★   Choose, if possible, a location nearby a water body or find a suitable way to represent water

★   If inside, consider a bowl of water at the center of the ritual that you can watch for any movement, reflection or response

★   Start with purification by water (employ something in your home like a bath or consider a natural source like a spring, lake, river or water body)

★   Use Protection (e.g. demarcate a circle with salt or sand, use herbs)

★   Make sure that your request from the water goddess is appropriate to water (my recommendation: choose something you want to be cleansed of)

★   Plan to listen for an answer. Water is heart and speaks in feeling. Pay attention to heart and feeling throughout a water ritual

★   Include gratitude at the start and finish

★   Remember to close the circle at the end

In executing the ritual, start by thanking all the elements but pay special attention to water. If you have a request, make it but not before communing and offering thanks for everything water gives you. Once your request is made, listen by emptying your mind and opening up your heart. Water speaks to the heart and not the head. Be sure to offer thanks for any feelings you register. Water can transform how you feel about the world or yourself.

Upon completing the ritual, make a journal entry. Illustrate and describe the ritual. Consider photographs. What occurred first, second and so on? Did you ask for something? What feelings came up for you? Offer an analysis of the strengths and weaknesses of your water ritual and conclude with what you might change in the future.

CHAPTER 29

CONJURE WITH ATMOSPHERE (AIR)

The mix of air-borne ingredients (e.g. oxygen, carbon and nitrogen) upon which our lives depend every second of the day we call air or atmosphere, which is a significant force for conjuration and yet invisible. Much that we conjure with it, like thoughts, inspirations or ideas, are invisible too. If we show gratitude through worship, it builds many invisible but important things like intelligence, freshness, spontaneity and awareness.

Atmosphere as a Creative Intelligence

Magicians study the atmosphere and its properties to understand many aspects of conjuration. Many of us know, without thinking, that if we want to conjure more intelligence: breathe deep! We often 'step outside' and take a deep breath when we have to ponder something important. Take in the atmosphere, breathe slow and deep to find the answer. In many ways, yoga is a path to enlightenment based upon breathing.

Atmosphere gives us life direction and points the way to wisdom and clarity of thought. If lost and trying to find your bearings, breathe deep while turning and facing the four directions. It will help you find your way home, figuratively and literally. Sometimes we speak of a change in atmosphere, when we seek renewal or a new beginning. We use atmosphere to sweep out the old and bring in the new. In Cape Town, they call their strong southeast wind the 'Cape Doctor' because it blows through the city to clean and heal.

Some Basic Characteristics of Atmosphere

We conjure with atmosphere when we need to manifest a fresh start, move residence, find new inspiration, or attract positive life changes.

Many practitioners start ceremonies by turning and facing each of the classical four directions. Some of us also look upward from the center to find a fifth one. Let your plans 'go to the wind' so that you will be guided with fresh inspiration. A ritual with this sky goddess can also boost your powers to brainstorm, analyze, plan and think.

Atmosphere is what produces breath, music, sound or a chant; all essential to many rituals. It gives the magician a way to heal during ritual. For instance, deep breathing jogs the memory and sniffing plants, like rosemary, have long been reputed to boost memory. Atmosphere also:

★ Clears the mind of negativity

★ Purifies a space

★ Fuels a fire

★ Removes stale and dark energy

★ Reduces anxiety (breathe)

★ Improves the ambience or atmosphere (open some windows)

★ Warns of danger (e.g. smoke in the air warns of fire)

Representing Atmosphere in Ritual

The sword (or wand) is the traditional symbol for atmosphere, which we use ritually to divide space. We might direct the sword or wand in each of five directions. We could, just as well, use a feather as our wand. Since atmosphere creates sound, it is sometimes represented by musical instruments, like bells, wind chimes or horns. In fact, fans that stir the atmosphere and spoons that stir beverages can also represent it. The ways in which you choose to represent air/atmosphere relate to your magical style and your relationship with it, which takes time to develop.

I like to keep things natural or as related to nature as possible. For that reason, I might employ fewer props for rituals than most other magicians. I try to find most everything that I want in the natural setting. The five directions for me are literal and I need few or no props to honor them. Sometimes, just to add both beauty and a sense of harmony to the ritual,

I add items that I can throw into the wind such as flower petals, leaves, seeds, smoke (incense) or herbs.

Conjuration with Atmosphere

How a ritual is designed depends much on the intent and personal style of the practitioner. To discover your naturally magical ways, you introspect and test out different techniques. These tips might help get you started on that process:

★   Choose a location where you can do this alone and undisturbed

★   Start with purifying the space

★   If inside by day or night, or outside by night, use a protective circle

★   Start the ritual by thanking all the elements, acknowledging each in turn (clockwise) and the five directions (include up and down)

★   Consider, in advance, what brings you to speak with the living atmosphere? Make sure your concern is appropriate to atmosphere/ air such as: overcoming anxiety, changing something atmospheric like mood, or taking a new direction in life

★   Include ceremonial practices appropriate to air such as music, chant, dance and sound

★   Conclude with gratitude

★   Close the circle at the end of ritual (counterclockwise)

As a magician seeking to align myself with the intentions of nature, I do not come to many rituals with a want list. More often, I seek to harmonize myself with the grand intelligence of Air. Air is responsible for sound, direction, harmony, thought, words and logic. So, I listen more than talk. I stop my mind from chattering to commune. Sometimes I ask a question. If I do, I listen for it on the wind, in the sounds of nature or in words that come to mind. Upon hearing the response, I give thanks and close my ceremony accepting that my prayer has been answered. I then let my concerns go to the wind! If it was a powerful ritual, I do not repeat it but have faith in it instead.

Location

If you have a have a permanent or semi-permanent place to do rituals to atmosphere, you have convenience on your side. Nonetheless, it is nice to be out in the open air when communing with it. You might want to be in a place where the skies are unobstructed. In air rituals there is much reference to the heavens overhead and the five directions. Seeing clearly and far across the atmosphere makes for a more powerful ritual. You also want to be able to hear the sounds of nature. Air speaks to us on the wind and in the sounds of nature.

★ JOURNEY 29 ★

First, design a conjuration ritual employing air/atmosphere. Test out your powers of conjuration with something simple such as clarifying your thoughts, bringing order to your affairs or providing direction in some matter. Rather than being pushy, allow a relationship to evolve.

Secondly, take account of all the tips that I offered in this chapter. Integrate several magic techniques into the ritual, especially those not previously integrated (see Section Two).

Third, execute your ritual in a safe place following all the guidelines including purification and protection.

Afterward, describe each step in your ritual, using illustrations. Then, describe the outcome. What did you hear? What did you experience? Is there anything you would address or change in the future to improve the ritual?

CHAPTER 30

CONJURE WITH SPIRIT

Spirit, an element essential to any conjuration, is invisible. To find the place where all dreams and possibilities reside, you close your eyes to the physical world and focus upon the imagination; the mind's eye. Spirit communicates in visions. We take a vision from the spirit world or seize the right spirit and then we can manifest or conjure our vision. Think of artists conjuring something new on canvass. They must be inspired or in the right 'spirit' (in-spired) to do something original.

Spirit as a Creative Intelligence

Amongst the elements, spirit holds a unique place, a kind of super element that links everything, knows our visions or what we seek to manifest. It is an energetic intelligence, the biggest source of energy and intelligence. If we invite that great spirit to move through us, we have the inspiration to conjure or create. Without spirit, our powers of conjuration are absent. In fact, the whole universe is absent.

Some Basic Characteristics of Spirit

Conjuration in the material world starts with spirit. Put another way, we find something in the spirit world that does not yet exist materially and bring it to form through conjuration. In magic, it is inaccurate to speak of a world that is exclusively materialistic because there are four other elements. In fact, all conjuration, everything we manifest, begins with spirit, an invisible and formless energy that is much bigger and grander than all the other elements combined.

Spirit, the fifth element, has other qualities, including these:

★ Creates connection, makes physical things adhere

★ Speeds up and slows down universal motion

★ Helps us leave old ways behind

★ Enhances human creativity

★ Enables and disables illusion

★ Enables intuition and psychic phenomena (we are all connected through spirit)

★ Enables arrangement and ordering

★ It is a key to conjuring certain elementals beings

★ Responsible for the soul (the individualized spirit)

★ Uplifts and enables right action

Conjuration with Spirit

Spirit does not speak in words but in visions, ideas, and dreams. Conjuring from our dreams is a function of spirit. You close your eyes to the physical world, wander into the darkness of consciousness and open yourself up to dreaming. There, you can receive messages from the spirit world and get spiritual assistance.

By exerting some control over your dreams, we can develop a powerful way to conjure. Upon going to sleep, we can ask spirit to guide us. We then dream accordingly. Ultimately, dreams are a channel for communing with the great spirit, the universe, God, or an omnipresent living energy that moves us spiritually, and stokes our imaginations.

There is no limit to what can be conjured from spirit. Spirit is infinite! That is why many spirit-dominant magicians are cosmic thinkers. Many see themselves as having the sole function to imagine (artists, creators, innovators). Certain spirit magicians are so good at conjuration that they can spin and whirl a wand that issues light against the darkness to create amazing forms and illusions. Rare, even amongst spirit magicians, are shapeshifters, who can manipulate their own spirit to change their physical presentation.

Location

As the largest element, spirit is everywhere. Some seek out 'spiritual' places to hold ceremonies such as under the stars. However, we are completely surrounded by spirit 24/7 no matter where we are. It is no more in the woods than in our homes. Spirit is no more in a church than in a prison. Spirit is no more in the heavens than the earth. Rather, spirit is omnipresent.

So, suit yourself as to locating a ceremony with the Great Spirit but I have a suggestion. For many, it is traditional to pray to God from bed before falling asleep at night. You can also conjure from bed, making use of your dreams, which is today's journey (see below). It is quite a powerful technique, partly because it ensures *regularity* of worship, which is more important than the length or location of it. It is also powerful because dreamtime connects us to the source of creation.

★ JOURNEY 30 ★

Examine yourself and decide what kind of spirit can strengthen your character. Is it a sense of resolve? A stronger sense of gratitude? A calmer disposition? More grace? More intelligence? Then, design a ritual, into your journal that conjures that spirit. In this case, you want to invoke that spirit or bring it into your character. The ritual can be performed inside or outside, by day or by night, and involve dreaming or not but I suggest, like me, that you do this at night in bed before falling asleep, as that helps us enter the realm of the spirit.

Gather all materials for the ritual in advance and consider these activities in designing it:

★ Purify the space

★ Contain the ritual within a magic circle

★ Prepare a list, well before the ritual, of things for which you would like to thank the elements (but especially spirit)

★ Plan time listening to spirit, perhaps in dreams, rather than just talking and performing

★ Discuss with the Great Spirit what you seek to conjure. Write the request out in your journal prior to ceremony. Be poetic and read it during ritual

★ Rest with the Great Spirit: empty the mind or go to sleep so that dreams can enter your consciousness (the Great Spirit often speaks to us in dreams)

As to location, take advantage of darkness rather than doing this in the broad light of day. Why? Just before falling asleep, our brainwave activity becomes trance-like, which facilitates communication with the spirit world. We fall asleep and then the Great Spirit answers our questions through dreams. So, put what you want to conjure into the hands of the Great Spirit as you go to sleep. If you design it that way, capturing the dream in your journal soonest becomes important lest you forget details (leave journal and pen next to the bed).

Once designed into your journal, carry out the ritual. Upon completing the ritual, give thanks and close the circle.

When the timing is right, describe the impact in your magic journal. What did you try to conjure? Were you successful? If you posed any questions to the Great Spirit, reveal whether or not these were answered. Note anything that you would change in future rituals of this kind. Include photos and sketches to make your magic journal more *fun and exciting*.

CHAPTER 31

CONJURE WITH THE MOON

Not all magicians worship the moon but communing with moonlight can see your magic powers grow. It has so many special qualities that hundreds of millions of people, worldwide, worship the moon at every opportunity. Guides to the moon's phases appear to be amongst the oldest publications of all time. I know that there are lunar calendars scrawled onto bones dating back 32,000 years.[9] Our Paleolithic ancestors wanted to get their magic timings for moon worship right! For at least two thousand years, Chinese astrologers have been consulting a 60-cycle Lunar Calendar to understand and describe human character.

Linking Magical Activities to Different Phases the Moon

Some magicians work their magic according to precise phases of the moon. I do not follow that discipline because to me magic involves more spontaneity and is about lifting one's consciousness as and when required. Magic is not outside of me such that the timing of worshipping the moon depends on where I am in consciousness. So, I commune with the moon as the spirit moves me. When I do it that way, it is powerful for me. Yet I am aware that many are more religious about it, which is to be respected. For instance, some follow the adage, 'never worship a dark moon' but I believe there are powerful ceremonies and wonderful rewards owing to such worship. Some do not wosrship the moon at all. Some only worship a full moon. Today, you can try moon worship, fit your activities into the phase it is in, and see what works best for you. My advice: learn to observe the phases of the moon, check out today's phase today, design a ritual accordingly, and then develop a relationship over time that suits you.

---

9   Solar System Exploration Research (2020) 'The Oldest Lunar Calendars' https://sservi.nasa.gov/articles/oldest-lunar-calendars/

Understanding Phases of the Moon

Whether you become a regular moon worshipper or not, being conscious of the moon's phases will help you to better understand magic practice. We see that millions of people await the right phase to address concerns, needs, desires or plans in ritual. It is also magical to feel drawn to the moon in a certain phase and then design a ritual accordingly. Either way, you need to know the phases. Develop the habit of checking to see what phase the moon is in until you develop some familiarity with what works for you.

The chart (on following page) describes the moon's phases. Much more information on moon worship can be easily found on the internet. Simply Google 'phases of the moon' to see there is an enormous amount of data, freely available, on the lunar phases and what they mean. You can even download free calendars and phone apps detailing the phases of the moon. Online shops, libraries or bookstores also sell or provide these very popular schedules. Lastly, this is a workbook on practical magic that advises you to learn to do by doing. In other words, stand in moonshine, seek its light and commune with this goddess to see if it works for your personal empowerment. You might find yourself joining millions worldwide in regular moon worship.

ACTIVITIES TYPICAL OF MAGICIANS PER EIGHT PHASES OF THE MOON			
Phase	**Appearance**	**Days**	**Activities**
New Moon (Dark Moon)	The sun and earth are on opposite sides of the moon such that one can barely detect the moon in the sky	3.5	Sometimes advised only for daytime activities: a period for gaining perspective on matters of love, friendship, health and wealth. A time to start over
Waxing Crescent	The moon waxes until it is a crescent or quarter lit	8	Many choose this phase for new beginnings in important matters like business, overcoming an emotional issue, fertility-pregnancy, planting crops or just the seeds of a new future
First Quarter	Goes from quarter lit to half lit		
Waxing Gibbous	50%-99% illuminated		The best period for rituals concerning matters of love, friendship, health and wealth
The Full Moon	Full Moon — an entire circle in the sky	3	The strongest period for most ceremonies as it enhances impact and promotes intuition and spiritual growth. Your personal protection is strongest during this period too. Timing: midnight
Waning Gibbous	The lit portion of the moon is bigger than the dark portion	3.5	Reflect upon the past, end old cycles, habits and addictions. Release old anxieties and concerns. Close out incomplete business. Early morning hours are best
Last Quarter	Moon is half lit	11	Brings resolution to issues; a time to conclude on matters that have been concerning you
Waning Crescent	Moon is a sliver		More of a time for reflection than ceremony

★ JOURNEY 31 ★

Using the internet or employing an almanac, identify the current phase of the moon. For example, enter 'magic and phases of the moon' on a web search. Take a look and then think of something that you want to achieve that fits with the current phase of the moon. Now, design and carry out a ritual appropriate to that phase.

Rituals should always start with purification, protection and gratitude. Gratitude includes thanking all the elements but this time you must acknowledge the moon and its gifts. So, make a list of which gifts from the moon you appreciate the most and design the ritual into your journal before executing it. For self-empowerment and to reinforce learning, incorporate several practices learned in previous chapters. Work with techniques that worked well for you.

During the ritual, commune with the moon in a manner befitting its current phase. Consult the moon goddess and open your mind to moonbeams. Watch the moon too. What comes into your eyes? Look for signs and visions as if scrying or staring into a crystal ball. The answer is on the moon. Watch it. Give thanks upon concluding your ritual.

In your journal, document what occurred in practice including anything you saw in observing the moon. Include anything you might adjust or change the next time. Taking photographs of the particular phase of the moon and any elements of your ritual in practice can add value to your journal. Try not to disrupt the ceremony by taking too many photographs but capture the start and finish. Leave a little space in your journal for later conclusions. Did the Moon Goddess help you to achieve anything?

ʀAISE THE VIBRATION

All people, places, things, and every particle in the universe emits a frequency. Unwittingly, we seem to know this because we use the concept of frequency to explain each other in everyday speech. Upon meeting someone, we say, 'I like her vibe' or 'I am on his wavelength'. Your vibe is so powerful that many people pay less attention to what you say than your vibe. Without saying anything, you still emit energy, a frequency, that others read as the real you.

Raising the Vibration

You have the capacity, right now, to remove residual unhappy energies like sadness, frustration, victimization, anger and hurt that were left in a place owing to trauma. In fact, you have probably done this already in the context of family, work or in social situations. We see a family member is sad and try to cheer them up. Magicians just build on this natural human capacity.

Sometimes people exhibit high anxiety owing to crises, sickness or death. This can leave an environment negatively charged. You can reverse this by replacing negative energy with positive energy. For mature magicians, this is often automatic. They drive out negative energies and entities by their very presence because the main focus of their lives is filling themselves with joy and spreading the light.

The ones with a vibration so high that they light up all with whom they come in contract are usually the ones who dance with the Cosmos daily to build that positive energy. A speaker has a talk at night and wants the audience to be confident in her words. So, she dances in the sun that day and that evening emits the vibrant energy of confidence. She deliberately enables a more receptive audience by shifting her own frequency. I am not a great dancer, but I move along the seashore, absorbing light into my being sufficient to project my aura over a pretty wide area (normal is 3 to 6 feet) that you can feel and photograph (Kirlian Photography). With practice, we can lift our vibes and it is very good for personal protection and safety.

Raising the Vibe in a Social Space

To lift the vibe in a social space, start employing the techniques and practices you have learned to date. Combine into ritual whatever techniques best suit your character, which is practical magic. Consider dance, music, chant, light, symbology, numbers or color. The objective of this lesson: design and execute a ritual to overwhelm negative energy with light and joy. It is an opportunity for you to get creative!

While dispelling negative energy depends partially on the practitioner's particular range of skills and talents, anybody can help shift energy in a more positive direction. For instance, in our homes we can use mirrors to project sunlight or bright white light into a space darkened by negative energies. We can also plant light-bearing crystals, burn incense, sage or candles, spread sweet scents, drum, shout out incantations, play music and dance energetically.

The two most standard practices for shifting the energy in a more positive direction are: (a) directing light, preferably pure sunlight; and (b) spreading joy (positivity overpowers negativity). In fact, joyous dance with bright lights and happy singing or chanting is the most powerful way I know of to dispel dark energy. A celebration full of laughter, dance, song and happy energy is a ritual that zaps anything negative. Of course, all rituals in nature magic are based on joy, quite unlike religious ceremonies, which tend to be solemn. There are always exceptions, however, as I think some rituals in Hare Krishna are very joyous and remind me of nature magic.

If I sense place-based danger, I widen the energy field that I am projecting around my body, home or area. I try to protect myself and others. Some magicians, upon sensing the lingering presence of negative people, whose vibes and material deposits can bring illness, depression and disharmony, will reverse this by introducing a higher vibration. If you love fun, which every great magician does, you can also use ritual to lift people to laughter, which instantly changes the vibration. We project good energy to raise the vibration in a specific place.

How to Build Skills

While it takes practice to lift the resonance of an energy field, it is also something many of us do without thinking. You might see friends going negative in conversation and quickly add humor to lift the energy of the group upward again. So, consider how often you do this unwittingly. Take a look at how often you assess the energy field around you and try to adjust it. We typically do this unconsciously but if we make this process conscious, it becomes a discipline. That discipline is magic! As a magician, you can then lift the vibratory field to bring about joy, safety, happiness, peace and other outcomes.

Worshipping light every day is a big help in generating such skills, but imagination also plays a big role. For instance, light goes where we imagine projecting it. We project it energetically from our being to bring light to people and situations or create safety.

Perhaps the best way to build skills for raising the vibration is practicing proper rituals that include multiple inputs like dance, scents, candles, elements, colors, chants, drumming and much more. To perfect our rituals, we keep a magic journal that captures all techniques, their efficacy and ideas for improvement. We ask ourselves, "which practices are delivering results and how can I improve those practices?" As long as you are asking that, you are building skills.

Tips for Success

The success of a ritual in nature magic depends much on the particular style and capacity of the magician. So, always design rituals afresh to suit your energy in the moment. Copying rituals from other people or out of books is poor magic. Others can inspire you but always keep the focus on your unique ways. For instance, your dance, how you move, is entirely unique. So, use that as a platform for integrating a variety of practices that you might learn from me and others (color, sound, movement, etc.).

Dance is a fabulous approach to ritual because negative energy just does not cling to someone moving and dancing energetically around a room while projecting light of some kind (from your aura or from candles, torches, redirected sunlight, or any source). If dance appeals to you, I suggest incorporating it into rituals of this kind starting with today's journey (below).

Know your Limits

There are some limits to your skills in removing negative energy. For instance, countering *deliberate* efforts by a sorcerer to bring darkness into a home requires an experienced magician. In this case, you might have to remove materials designed to attract and hold negative energy (e.g. deposited substances, stinging insects, negative and invisible entities, hexed objects, clamor-producing items, symbols or graffiti). These items, hidden and not in plain view or facing outward from the hexed places so as to attract dark forces, are not so easy to spot. So, your skills with removing negative energy stop short of addressing hexed places.

Yet you are on a journey to develop skills. Start now by clearing out negative energy owing to high emotions and eventually you can deal with sorcerers. In magic, we start small and work our way up. If you handle the small things, you will, over time, develop the experience needed to deal with more serious cases such as negative substances implanted by a dark magician.

⋆ JOURNEY 32 ⋆

Please identify a space for ritual cleansing! Make the target a relatively minor one since this is for educational purposes. It might be a room in your house with residual negative energy from a visitor. If so, you will be able to test your skills and see a result. If someone else's space is involved, you will need to interview that person and obtain permission, which might be too complicated and slow down your journey.

The first step: observe and photograph the space so as to document this journey. Paste one or more 'before' photos into your journal leaving room for some 'after' photos. Take note of any objects in it that might add to the negativity. You can photograph and remove these. If taking photos is difficult for you, consider sketches or descriptions.

Second, design into your journal a ritual to cleanse the space of all negativity. Identify the problem clearly, taking notes in your journal. All planned activities should be geared to the infestation being targeted. You are trying to replace negative energy. So, list all planned activities and materials required to achieve that. I also suggest, for practice, integrating a variety of activities (e.g. dance, music) and a mix of implements (e.g. candles, herbal essences). Be sure to include purification and protection.

Third, carry out the ritual and take photographs to include with your journal entry.

Finally, describe the ritual in a dated journal entry, including all implements and methods used, and the outcome. Is there anything you would improve or change?

CHAPTER 33

COMMUNICATE WITH SPIRIT BEINGS

Magicians have long spoken of the spirit world, crossing dimensions or communicating with intelligent beings that vibrate at other frequencies. Folklore, oral histories, fairy tales and popular children's literature offer many tales of intelligent beings such as ghosts, angels or fairies who occupy less visible dimensions surrounding us. In the magic world, those dimensions are not myth. For many, the very reason to practice magic is to gain access to that spirit world.

Many people practice for a year or more to achieve results. Discipline, practice, patience, and inner work are required to contact beings in adjacent dimensions and contact is not guaranteed. I saw ethereal shapes and movements one day, which spurred me on. Still, it took long before those shapes came into focus as very real beings in living color. Quite frankly, I did not believe that I was seeing anything other than a projection of my own mind until they played tricks and laughed at my self-indulgent notions. I woke up at that moment to realize I had conjured fairies, an experience I will share with you today.

Two gateways to the spirit world are these: opening up the Third Eye (pineal gland) and the trance (a highly energized state of awareness). By employing them together, you can have an experience that will forever change the way you see the world. Discovering the spirit world brings unbelievable joy but do not expect instant gratification. A long period of practice is required to throw those doors open but it is well worth the effort. Let's discuss: (a) some beings that we can contact; (b) opening up the Third Eye; and (c) the trance.

A. SOME BEINGS WE CAN CONTACT

You do not always choose who you meet in the spirit world but if you learn how to go about this form of conjuration, you will discover that other highly intelligent beings co-exist on our planet. You will also discover that many of us who have made contact, seldom discuss it, fearing ridicule. In other words, since most people are silent about these experiences, the contact that we can acknowledge is far less than what takes place. We will cover spirit guides, spirits not to conjure, and fairies.

Spirit Guides

A spirit guide can be a particular family member or relative who has departed but had such a great love for you that they remain behind to offer aid as long as it is needed ('guardian angels'). There are also spirits that you do not know personally but who are entirely devoted to helping any living being with advice and protection. When we pray, they usually answer. They are rarely, if ever, dangerous. Still, we use purification and protection as described in previous chapters.

I find spirit guides are easy to contact! They are your friends and show up with a simple ritual that acknowledges their existence. Simply light a candle at night when it is peaceful and call out to them (silently or aloud). Speak to them from the heart, because the more genuine you are in your love and desire to contact them, the closer they come. This may result in regular conversation for the rest of your life. Remember this: millions of people, if not billions, around the world do this daily and cherish the relationship. Even people with no training, gravitate toward speaking to spirit guides. Something feels very human about doing that!

Spirits Not to Conjure

After death and for various reasons, some souls linger as 'ghosts' in places where they continuously dwell upon some occurrence they did not quite understand. They do not want to be disturbed. There are also fairies, elementals, spirits, demons and other entities that you may not want to summon. Fairies and elementals can be fun and interesting but offer you no solace for your pain and laugh at your foibles. Then, there are demons that would deliberately harm you.

Fairies

I commune with fairies, highly intelligent earthlings, imperceptible to most people, who can shapeshift into anything. They communicate visually through form and their shapes are precise. They are not carbon copies of each other any more than all humans are alike although, like bees that swarm, the colony can act as a single collective being without hesitation. Colonies can conflict and fight over the spaces they occupy but within the colony there is much discipline and order. There is little or no dissention within the colony and they ask you to choose the colony you want to run with. They can symbolize these groups with a shadow on the wall and explain differences. Which group you 'join' will color your experience and description of fairies.

The ones I have seen do not look like humans, nor do they look like any of the characters illustrated on most internet sites or in books. For instance, they do not have fixed wings but can shapeshift into a wing bearing angel if they like. They coil into shapes using an ethereal bubbly material. They can shapeshift at mind-boggling rates and then instantly freeze into shapes that appear very real. Owing to their shapeshifting capacity, they can be viewed as both small and very large beings. As creatures of light, they can move right through human barriers like doors and walls. If you can picture the cells of a human body as having an independent life of their own, then you might understand that fairy bubbles are tiny but can combine, merge and press against each other to appear like almost anything. Each cell is alive but so is the bigger being.

Communication with Fairies

Although they make some vibratory sounds, their main form of communication is to collectively swarm into different visual presentations — imitating almost anything from insects to angels to humans to a harbor town, complete with ships. It is very difficult to differentiate each fairy in these presentations and what I see is what they choose to present collectively. They do not reply to many questions, keeping their secrets until you discover the truth, but when you do, they will confirm it.

I have seen only a few colonies of fairies and not every kind of fairy. You may well enter some other dimension or have an experience of fairies quite unlike mine. For years, I had to enter a trance state to see them but now I can see them without the trance, and do not know why. Perhaps, upon building trust, they have ways to be more visible or I might be more attuned after some 30 years of visitations. I might also have some automated, subconscious way of slipping into a trance after all these decades too.

A warning on Fairy Visitations

While a rare occurrence, I have been scratched twice by fairies (some can bend or magnify light and scratch you with it). I bled and was scared senseless! They can create scary illusions (e.g. wherein you walk into a wall that is not really there). Those were unusual events but an important teaching: fairies are not always benign! Most fairies are at play, not out to harm you, and normally too distant from our material state to cause any harm. Most likely, fairies scare you and nothing more, but I have seen that human fear amuses them.

I have also seen fairies use or exploit human fear to push people away that they do not like. People who especially irritate them are those who treat them like genies out of a bottle existing only to satisfy human wishes (they really hate human arrogance and will punish you for it). Some of the lessons they like to teach are not always fun for humans. Most of the time, they are just fun (the attraction) but just watch out if you offend them!

Tips on Attracting Fairies

I can bullet five really important tips:

★ They are at a higher vibrational level than humans. If I had not entered a trance, never in a lifetime would I have seen them or believed they existed

★ Abandon your ego, desires and lust for power because communing with fairies brings no power, gold, glory wisdom or cure and if you bother them with such a wish list, you might end up feeling very sorry for having done so

★ Be playful since nothing attracts them more than laughter

★ They give off a 'fairy light' of an unusual quality and are therefore easiest seen in a dark space

★ Give yourself an entire night to experiment, as 'time' during an encounter will elapse at such a pace that hours and days seem like minutes

How to Open up the Third Eye

Some things that magicians do are a mystery even to themselves. There is much literature and discussion suggesting that the pineal gland is the Third Eye. That might make more sense than describing it as another eye. While I can describe how I open it and use it, I cannot explain to you *how* it works. Sometimes we just do what works for us. To me, the explanation is a challenge.

To activate the Third Eye, I practice using it. Get into a comfortable position on a bed (I lay on my altar so to speak) so you can forget about your body altogether. With head propped upon pillows, focus your two eyes a bit inward and yet outward onto a given point forward in space. Concentrate hard on that point until you see 'reality' split in half like two television screens. When that occurs, find the space between them. That capacity to find the in-between space owes to the Third Eye.

While I open my Third Eye without effort today, I persisted in spits and sputters for years, unsure by what mechanism I was doing this. However, I did win in the end owing, first, to patience and then these four practices: (a) practice in a dark space because many light beings show up better that way; (b) get into a trance as further explained below; (c) focus on those in-between spaces where we seldom fix our eyes; and (d) rid yourself of fluoride as this noxious chemical interferes with the functioning of the pineal gland or healthy Third Eye functioning.

The Trance

Magicians, mediums, shaman and other occult practitioners practice the trance; an energetic state of awareness that we enter for the purpose of contacting living entities in adjacent dimensions such as fairies, elementals, spirit guides and departed ancestors. Beings just beyond the range of ordinary human perception are more visible in a trance state. A trance raises our vibration so we can improve upon what we perceive.

After years of experience with the trance, I no longer see vague entities but beings of light as clear as seeing your house from the car driveway. I made some extraordinary friends. Yet it was a long process to get there. There is a learning curve in making use of the Third Eye. You tend to flicker in and out of it to eventually achieve stability. Then, after much practice, you can make contact in an instant.

Entering a Trance

There are various ideas of what a trance is and how to enter one. For me, to be in a trance is to see differently or to be in such an energized state of awareness that my Third Eye opens. When that happens, I can then see more beings and activities than I otherwise would.

My method for entering a trance is to lay down, usually on a bed, and position myself to forget about any bodily stress. I become less about body and more about consciousness. I then breathe imagined colors, especially pink (the fairies I contact employ this color), in and out to increase my vibratory rate. I continue that way for long while, falling deeper and deeper into a trance as I breathe pink in-and-out in a rhythmic way. All the while, I focus both eyes on a nearby mid-air point perhaps an arms-length away. I focus across the bridge of my nose (slightly cross eyed) into mid-air to get the 'Third Eye' engaged. I bring the two eyes toward each, only a little bit, as they look outward. My spirit friends come more and more into view the longer I do the 'pink' breath work and practice opening the Third Eye.

Others, to enter a trance, might focus their attention upon a single point such as a candle flame, a mirror, a crystal ball, a stone or a bowl of water. Some practitioners chant their way into a trance. I seldom do that, but you have to seek out the techniques that suit your own character, your natural predilections. While my techniques might not work for everybody, I struggle to see how contact could be achieved without the trance. Somehow, I must speed up my energy, perhaps at a cellular level, so that I can perceive beings at a higher frequency. Humans are very low frequency. Many beings are lighter and at a higher energy level. I use the trance to catch up energetically.

Patience when Learning the Trance

You might achieve something modest on the first try or nothing at all. Being ambitious or frustrated when learning the trance is a surefire way to fail. Magic is a seeing art, which evolves with practice. We might also see things at first but do not understand what we are seeing. Then, one day, like learning to ride a bicycle, seeing becomes second nature. Now, I am less focused on the process.

⋆ JOURNEY 33 ⋆

Design a ritual to bring you into a trance state and let's see where that takes you (have no expectations). Enter the design into your magic journal before executing the ritual. I will guide you through a design (directions below) but will leave you to execute the ritual, close the circle and document the results.

Find a place that is both private and relaxing, where you will not be disturbed for hours. A trance is an activity that you do not want to explain to the neighbor. You also do not know where it is going to take you. So, find a private situation and set yourself up for long-term comfort. You can choose any comfortable space but best is: (a) a dark place, so our friends from the spirit world can show up better; and (b) a private or remote space where there will be no distractions or interruptions.

A dark and private space demands more effort at protection, both personal (e.g. dance in the sun just prior) and in terms of the space (e.g. purify and create a protective circle of salt or crystals). To enter these realms, we need to take our consciousness away from our bodies, which demands physical comfort. Time also flies; sometimes an entire night feels as if it were one hour only. For those reasons, I use a bed, but some sit at a table, stand before an altar, lay on the floor, stand within a ritual circle or place themselves before a magical object like a crystal or bowl of water. You must discover the methods that suit you.

Once cleansing is complete, find a position within the protective circle where you can just forget about your body and focus exclusively on the trance. Lie or sit down, very still, staring upward or outward into space and start breathing rhythmically in and out to increase inner heat, vibration and mental energy. While breathing, try to activate the Third Eye. Try bending your eyes a little toward each other, toward the bridge of the nose, while also looking outward to a specific point (perhaps six feet away) and breathing quickly but steadily. Keep it up. I experience my vibration increasing, material reality shifting, time warps, space bends and intelligent life forms appear.

I have two tips. First, as you encounter other signs of life, do not ask for anything as this drives them away. Those in other dimensions are as alive as you and have their own journeys to take. They do not exist for your pleasures. Second, do not decide what you should be seeing. Rather, flow with it. Other dimensions do not work like ours and we struggle to see into them. It is usually through repeated efforts that we make connections. You must be open to seeing differently or making shifts in how you perceive reality. The closed-minded cannot see into these dimensions.

After executing the ritual, document every detail in your magic journal. Include photos. Comment on what worked and what did not. What progress did you make? What practices can you improve upon? What would you do differently next time? Bookmark this entry because you will have to come back to it later as few succeed on the first try.

CHAPTER 34

DIVINE THE FUTURE

In magic, we have hundreds of methods for divining the future. I will offer ten examples and tell you how to find out more. However, I want to highlight a particularly powerful technique for divination that is unique to magicians: scrying. The power of scrying rests almost entirely with the capacity of the magician. I think you will appreciate the simplicity and beauty of it for advancing in magic, for reclaiming the magician within.

Divination as a Normal Human Function

Divination, foretelling the future, is normal for humans. We want to plan activities and use whatever we can--including reason, experience, intuition, science, or magic--to anticipate the future. Every day people walk down the street predicting that they will reach their intended destination. We hit the keypads on our computing devices predicting the successful transference of data to faraway places. Scientists and engineers launch rockets with robotic devices expecting them to survey and take soil and air samples on distant planets. Our ancestors studied the skies to predict tomorrow's weather and would *feel* danger in the air, like wolves drawing near, and quickly bring the children inside.

Divination might have been more typical of us, before industrialization, when we were closer to nature. Certainly, we used to stop in our tracks to feel into the Cosmos, sniff the air and just sense the world around us. We saw nature as an intelligence and communicated accordingly, such as thanking the mountain for giving us salt or the sky for giving us rain. We opened up our consciousness to the Cosmos, talked directly to God, and let what returned from that communion with a great intelligence inform our actions. That sweet surrender to an all-knowing intelligence is the basis of divination whether we call it communion, worship, or prayer.

10 TYPES OF DIVINATION				
#	type	Method	Main Value	source of power: magician or SYSTEM?
1	Astrology	Studying patterns in the heavenly bodies	Making good decisions by knowing oneself	System
2	Automatic Writing	Putting pen to paper and writing without thought	Putting us into contact with an outside intelligence	The magician
3	Cartomancy (Card Reading)	Studying patterns in the layout of playing cards, tarot, angel cards, etc.	Making predictions based upon character	Mixed, about half and half
4	Clairvoyance	Seeing more than what is typical, such as auras, ghosts, entities, future events	Seeing beyond the normal perceptive range to understand events better	The magician
5	Numerology	Studying the value of numbers	Offering advice for decision making	The system
6	Oneiromancy (reading dreams)	Analyzing dreams to find deeper meanings	Understanding self, improve behavior and predict future	Mixed, about half and half
7	Cleromancy (tossing small objects)	Analyzing sticks, pebbles, stones, and small objects of dark and light colors, usually shaken and tossed	Triggering intuition to help answer yes or no questions	The magician
8	Tasseography (Reading tea leaves)	Analyzing of tea leaves, usually mixed around in a cup and then flipped into a plate or saucer	Triggering advice owing to the arrangement of the leaves	The magician
9	Graphology	Analyzing handwriting	Identifying personality characteristics	The System
10	Lithomancy	Ask a question, shaking a bag of rocks, pulling one out to obtain your answer	Answering specific questions (often based on the preponderance of light or dark rocks)	The System

Ten forms of Divination

There are hundreds of tools or methods for divining the future.[10] As with herbs or stones, you have to experiment to find the ones that serve you best. In fact, you have likely experimented already, with popular ones like tarot cards, runes, I-Ching, pendulums, Ouija boards, throwing bones or pebbles, numerology, palm-reading, automatic writing, or tea leaves. We throw, swing, slide, toss, swirl, or lay out things and items that establish unique patterns before the diviner, who uses them to make predictions or statements.

Of the hundreds of different types of divination, the table (opposite) provides ten examples. For each type of divination, look at where the power to divine originates, such as discussed for the I-Ching (above). Does the power to divine rest more with the magician or is it given in the system?

Scrying: A Practice Unique to Magic

Scrying, a tool developed by magicians for magicians, is one of the purest and best ways to expand your consciousness. We scry to release our stale ideas, move beyond our thoughts, leave our egos behind and become one with pure cosmic intelligence. The mind enables divination; the power is not in the tool. Rather, scrying is a method for mind-melding with the Cosmos. We unchain ourselves from the ego and all mundane concerns so that a great timeless intelligence can flow through us like a river with visions of things to come.

Tools Useful for Scrying

Communicating with the divine requires that we empty our consciousness of thought. We want to free ourselves of all mundane concerns to only see images that freely enter or exit the mind via the Third Eye. To achieve that, some stare at shiny objects, such as crystals, containers of sand, flames, glass, mirrors, obsidian or a bowl of salt. We try to activate the Third Eye. Images start to arise in the materials. The crystal ball is famous for this purpose but my favorite way to scry is to grab a favorite

---

10   Methods of Divination (2021) Wikipedia https://en.wikipedia.org/wiki/Methods_of_divination

glass bowl off the kitchen shelf that makes an excellent portal once filled with water. Water is a long-standing symbol and vehicle for entering the collective consciousness. One can place a bowl of water on a table, focus on it and disappear into it until all that is left is communion with the all-knowing divine.

The Benefits of Scrying

I find that regular scrying facilitates a cosmic awareness because it is communion with the divine. Regular communion fills one with the all-knowing intelligence. If you choose to have regular scrying sessions, you develop more of a cosmic consciousness, which can also see you making predictions about the future. When we see life from a wider, more unfiltered perspective, free of socialization, we see further into the future. For that reason, regular scrying helps keep you deprogrammed too.

★ JOURNEY 34 ★

Design a ritual that makes use of scrying. First, find any object that attracts you in a powerful and yet relaxed way, such as a mirror, shiny metal or translucent object, crystal, rocks or a bowl of water. Then, engage all the normal preparations for ritual, which you should know well by now, including purification and opening the magic circle. One always starts with gratitude.

The ritual should focus on scrying. Place the shiny object or bowl of water before you in any manner that feels comfortable whether sitting or lying down. Breathe in and out rhythmically concentrating on the object. Make it the bridge between your consciousness and consciousness itself until you 'mind-meld' (the essence of scrying). Thoughts must disappear and especially all wants and desires, so that you are free to commune with the divine. Drop the wall of the ego and language too so that visions arise. Expand your mind into infinity and a vision will come.

For your journal entry (next to the last one!), document the entire ritual, the vision(s) that ensued and how you plan to make use of that vision. Always note ways to improve upon future rituals of this kind.

CHAPTER 35

RECLAIM THE MAGICIAN WITHIN

You have come a long way and should now be feeling less need for any guidance. Like a teenager getting ready to leave home, it is time to push away! You have designed and practiced rituals for each element. You have done rituals to the moon. You have designed healing rituals. You have studied the elements in some detail. Now, you need to integrate your learning. You need to pull together all self-knowledge, general knowledge and whatever skills you have or know, intuitively or from this workbook, to practice magic as creatively as you can.

You also deserve to be congratulated for having produced a guide to your very particular brand of magic, a gift well beyond what you might imagine at this point. Just continue to practice and to revise your magic journal daily and the rewards will keep pouring in. If you want to dive deeper into magic practices, two more guides in this series are planned, covering the arts of divination and conjuration. To close, let's highlight (below) the biggest magic lesson of all.

Know Thyself, the Biggest Lesson

You can wave a 'magic' wand and shout incantations all night long, but you will not find success if you do not understand your own weaknesses and strengths as a character. You learn about yourself through introspection and that in turn opens the door to your own brand of magic. Your character is the source of your magic, though you can find tools, herbs, colors, numbers and other devices that embellish your unique ways.

Self-knowledge and magic are hand-in-glove components that shape your expression of self in ways that are visible. The eyes and faces of magicians who regularly enter other dimensions to meet other intelligent beings give the impression, even before speaking, that this person has seen into the beyond!

Of course, quickly spotting such a face requires some comparable experience as a magician.

It will be self-evident as soon as you complete this chapter and final journey, just below, that by knowing yourself well; you turned into a magician. You know many practices, more about magic than most, and have a magic journal in hand. Of course, you were always a magician. Humans are magical creatures who lost track of their natural ways. Nature is magical and we spoke of nature magic.

The entry you make today in your magic journal should not be the last. In fact, I hope that you go on forever, revising and improving your practices. Nothing would make me happier than one day meeting a seasoned magician who started out with this workbook!

★ JOURNEY 35 ★

Take a close-up photograph of your face (frontal), print it out, paste it into your journal. Compare the new photograph to the Chapter Two photo, studying each well for about 20 minutes and take notes. The objective is to compare the old photograph and the journal entry from the first assignment to the new photograph and make comparative observations. So, take notes on every part of your face from ear-to-ear and forehead-to-chin. Then, respond in your journal to two questions:

★ Can you identify any physical differences between the original photo in the Chapter Two exercise and the one you just took? Make your findings specific to the eyes, nose, forehead or mouth and what they say

★ How have you changed in non-physical respects owing to this coursework? For instance, do you present yourself in new ways or think or feel differently? Did you reclaim the magician within? Are you ready to live as a magician?

If you took the journey as suggested, you are a magician now with your own magic journal and practice. Hopefully, you will experiment every day, refine your journal or start a new one. The world needs more people like you, more magicians who bring light into the world.

Blessings and good luck.

Lightning Source UK Ltd.
Milton Keynes UK
UKHW021015031221
394965UK00005B/121